Divided Paths | Common Ground

The Founders Series

Divided Paths | Common Ground

The Story of Mary Matthews and Lella Gaddis,

Pioneering Purdue Women Who

Introduced Science into the Home

by
Angie Klink

Purdue University Press, West Lafayette

Library of Congress Cataloging-in-Publication Data
Klink, Angie, 1959-
   Divided paths, common ground : the story of Mary Matthews and Lella
Gaddis, pioneering Purdue women who introduced science into the home
/ Angie Klink.
      p. cm. ~ (Founders series)
   Summary: "The book is about the accomplishments for women achieved
by Purdue University's first dean of the School of Home Economics, Mary
Matthews, and the first state leader of Home Demonstration, Lella
Gaddis"~ Provided by publisher.
   Includes bibliographical references and index.
   ISBN 978-1-55753-591-7 (pbk.)
   1. Matthews, Mary Lockwood, b. 1882. 2. Gaddis, Lella.
3. Purdue University~Faculty~Biography. 4. Women deans (Education)~
United States~Biography. 5. Purdue University~History~20th century. 6.
Home economics~Study and teaching (Higher)~United States~History~
20th century. I. Title. II. Series.

LD4672.K55 2011
378.0092'2~dc22
[B]

                                                                    2011001716

Cover design by Natalie Powell.
Back cover photograph by Jack Klink.

To Steve, Jack, and Ross, my common ground

Within these pages every night,
Brief memories of the day I write;
A little word, a single line,
Is jotted in this book of mine—
Not mighty deeds, just common things,
The tasks and pleasures each day brings.
And yet I hope that when I look
Over the pages of this book,
'Twill be (and, if so, I'm content)
The record of five years well spent.

–Eloise Wood, Ward's A Line A Day, Five Year Diary,
from the collection of Kate Gaddis (1923-1927;
1928-1932; 1933-1937)

Contents

Preface

Divided Paths, Common Ground is a rare occasion. It is a whisper from
the past as we are privy to the day-to-day details of a woman who lived
during the first part of the twentieth century. Bertha Kate Gaddis, a
teacher, wrote in her line-a-day diaries for forty years, recording the
minutiae of her world while also lifting up, like a bauble to the light,
the historic events in America that painted her backdrop. *Divided
Paths, Common Ground* invites the reader to pull up a kitchen chair and
sit down with Kate and her sister Lella Reed Gaddis, Indiana's first
state leader of home demonstration agents in Purdue's Department
of Agricultural Extension, and gather snippets of their lives that
swirled amid remarkable happenings in the United States from the
1910s to the 1940s. It was a time of startling change, especially for
women, and Kate's journals reveal how a small enclave of the country
experienced those changes.

Ultimately, this book is about Lella Reed Gaddis and her contem-
porary, Mary Lockwood Matthews, the first dean of the School of
Home Economics at Purdue University, but many layers of a bygone
era surround their life stories. Another extraordinary woman in *Divided Paths, Common Ground* is Mary's adoptive mother, Virginia Claypool Meredith, the first woman to serve on the Purdue University
Board of Trustees. In 1882, Virginia became a widow at age thirty-
three and chose to take over the operation of her late husband's 115-
acre ranch with prize shorthorn cattle and Southdown sheep. She was
a woman light years ahead of her time as a "lady farmer" and as a
late-in-life single mother.

I extend a thank you to Miriam Epple-Heath, the great-niece of
Lella and Kate Gaddis, for her insights into the personalities of her

aunts and entrusting me with Kate's diaries. The day Miriam handed me an old shoebox and I peered inside to see eighteen leather-bound journals, I had no idea of the historical significance and new friendship that waited within.

I also thank Eva Goble, dean emeritus of the School of Home Economics at Purdue University. Dean Goble invited me to lunch on several occasions, and her stories of the strivings of women in Indiana and at Purdue, along with her memories of Mary Matthews and Lella Gaddis, add an additional spark to *Divided Paths, Common Ground*. At this writing, the last time I met with Dean Goble, she told me she was "one hundred *and a half*." We were walking down the hall of her retirement home. She stopped, peered into the exercise room, and said, "Oh good. No one is in there. I'll come down later and workout."

Over a period of five months, I read Kate's diaries, sentence by sentence, day by day, year by year. The more I read, the more humbling became the experience of writing *Divided Paths, Common Ground*. Kate wrote her last lines in 1946 at Christmastime, and I read those final diary words sixty-four years later as the snow fell and my Christmas tree lights shimmered. *Divided Paths, Common Ground* depicts the lives and accomplishments of Lella Reed Gaddis, Bertha Kate Gaddis, Mary Lockwood Matthews, Virginia Claypool Meredith, and, in essence, all women of any time. Kate set this book aglow, pulling us along her timeline as we gather bits of lore along the way. I thank her, and I miss her.

—Angie Klink

There is a radiance where women move
Above small household tasks if they but see
Beyond the polished surface of old woods
The dazzling triumph of a living tree,
If they but see beyond the white, heaped flour—
Beyond the red, glassed jellies on a sill—
Wide joyous wheat fields laughing in the sun;
God's face above an orchard on a hill.

–Printed in *Lella Gaddis Portrait Presentation
Program, January 16, 1941*

Fork in the Road

It is the heart of the night. The stars and moon illuminate the dusty roads. Few gaslights burn at this hour. The Purdue Ag Boys hook up the team to the wagon and climb aboard. Time to take what they deem is rightfully theirs. The clop-clop of the horses and rumbling of the wagon break the silence of the campus as they make their way across State Street to Ladies Hall where, by day, the women students attend their home economics classes.

Once in the building, the Ag Boys find the woman's desk and files. To the wagon they carry the office furniture and each paper and record they believe should belong on "their side." They hurry aboard the wagon, give a yank to the reins, and the horses move the office of Miss Lella Gaddis, the new state leader of home demonstration, to the "Ag side."

The next day, Miss Gaddis reports to the Department of Agricultural Extension at Purdue University. She no longer works for the Department of Household Economics headed by Miss Mary Matthews. When Miss Matthews discovers her Home Demonstration Agent has been stolen from her, she is incensed. She believes the new position of state leader of home demonstration should be in her realm. The men in the Agricultural Department believe Lella Gaddis should work in the newly forming Extension Service.

It is then, in 1914, that the paths of Lella Reed Gaddis and Mary Lockwood Matthews are divided. Yet in the years to come, they will politely walk the same direction, intersect in the same circles, and forge new trails for women at Purdue and throughout Indiana, but always with watchful eyes upon one another.

⟶⬻⬻⟶

So weaves the story, the "mythology," told in 2010 by Dean Emeritus of the School of Home Economics Eva Goble, age one hundred. (Upon retirement, Lella Gaddis hired Dean Goble as her successor.) Did Lella know her office would be moved that clandestine night in 1914? "I'm sure she knew," Goble said. "She knew what was going on. The men controlled the money. Dean Matthews said, 'If I'm going to train these people (home economics leaders and students), it seems I should have the money in my budget.' Which was reasonable. The men didn't think so. It caused these two women to be full of animosity. They were always nice to each other, but they never missed an opportunity to give a little 'punch' now and then."

"That story is repeated around the state in every college I've attended," said Goble. "I attended Central Normal for two or three semesters. Guess what? The men came with horse and wagon and moved some of the college from some other county to Hendricks County."

The "story" really began when President Abraham Lincoln signed the first Land-Grant Act (originally the Morrill Act) on July 2, 1862. The creation of land-grant colleges such as Purdue University had a momentous bearing on the achievements of America, the start (slow as it was) of higher education, and the betterment of women and families.

The Land-Grant Act gave each state public lands that they could sell and use as an endowment to start a university to teach agriculture and mechanic arts. The purpose of these colleges was to educate more people in academic as well as practical pursuits. Home economics was included as part of agriculture.

Indiana's land-grant college had trouble finding a place to call home, as if no one wanted it. It was offered to several institutions that already existed, but they declined the proposal. Many people could not see how the teaching of agriculture and mechanical arts would be of interest to people or have much application.

To the rescue came the Lafayette merchant and banker John Purdue. He saw the great possibilities in such an institution. He offered Indiana $150,000 and eighty acres of land if they would put the university in Tippecanoe County, give it his name, and make him a lifelong trustee. His offer was accepted, and this is why Purdue University is one of few land-grant colleges in the country not named after a state.

In 1874, Purdue University opened to men only. Most lacked the prior education necessary to take college-level classes, so for the first couple of years only preparatory classes were taught. Although some agriculture subjects were offered, very few men took the courses. They probably thought they already knew how to farm. Women students were first admitted in the fall of 1875.

In 1882, William C. Latta, a graduate of Michigan State, was hired as a professor of agriculture. It was difficult to teach agriculture or domestic arts in those days because there were no textbooks, very little research had been done, and successful farming was mostly a matter of opinion.

In 1887, Congress passed the Hatch Act, which started the Agricultural Experiment Stations. The Agricultural Experiment Stations made research possible, and the facts gathered could be taken to farms and kitchen tables throughout the state.

Members of the Purdue University Board of Trustees established a Department of Agricultural Extension in 1911. The legislature made a very small appropriation for this department to begin informal education programs off-campus with field demonstrations for farmers, home management demonstrations for rural women, tomato clubs for girls, and corn clubs for boys. (Later absorbed into the 4-H movement, these clubs provided education on tomato canning for girls and corn growing methods for boys.) Academic and scientific knowledge could be carried directly to the people to change lives for the better, specifically creating happier and healthier lives for women and children. This was where Mary Matthews, a tall young woman, age twenty-nine, first appeared on the Purdue scene as an extension home economics instructor.

George I. Christie, then director of the Department of Agricultural Extension in Indiana, had discovered Mary while she was working in the extension field near Connersville where she lived with her adoptive mother, Virginia Claypool Meredith. University officials quickly recognized the capabilities of the gracious and charming young woman. In the first year, there were thirty-three "domestic science" demonstrations that reached some four thousand Indiana women.

The next year, Mary stayed on campus to teach home economics in the Purdue summer school. She was invited to join the School of Science staff, and in the fall of 1912, Mary became the first head of the School of Home Economics in Ladies Hall, a brick Victorian building with twin towers, a small veranda, and a metal fire escape that "crawled" up the exterior. Ladies Hall was combination boarding hall and classroom facility. Mary's task of creating a brand new department, finding qualified instructors, encouraging more women to attend college, and finding and retaining the necessary funds bestowed by the men in power proved a continual challenge throughout her career at Purdue.

Lella Gaddis was hired by Mary Matthews to teach in the 1914 Purdue summer school where she assisted in training the first home economics vocational teachers in Indiana. That year she also entered extension service in home economics, organizing extension work during its infancy. The night Lella was moved from Ladies Hall to Agricultural Extension, Mary knew the Ag Boys were at it again. They wanted her appropriations recently made possible by yet another governmental proclamation—the Smith-Lever Act.

Although extension work was already taking place, the Smith-Lever Act, signed by President Woodrow Wilson on May 8, 1914, authorized the organization of extension at the county, state, and federal levels. As a form of cost sharing, the act required matching funds from state and local sources. Thus, it became known as the *Cooperative Extension Service*. It was a partnership between the U.S. Department of Agriculture and the land-grant universities. Wilson called it "one of the most significant and far-reaching measures for the education of adults ever adopted by the government." The underlying philosophy of the system was to "help people help themselves" by "taking the university to the people."

Each state extension service is headquartered at a land-grant university and usually is closely associated with the Agricultural Experiment Station. This trio of entities—the land-grant university, Agricultural Experiment Station, and Cooperative Extension Service—makes for a uniquely American Institution that continues to influence countless lives.

While Lella Gaddis forged new ground traveling the state to "discover the needs of the people and devise a way to meet the needs" with her home base at Purdue's Agricultural Experiment Station, Mary Matthews was working on campus paving new roads for women as she established the new Department of Household Economics in the School of Science. Women did not yet have the right to vote in political elections. The positions held by Lella (a state leader of home demonstration, thanks to the Smith-Lever Act) and Mary (department head for a land-grant university) were made possible by a government in which they had no say.

The personalities of these two women were very different. Lella was "a real sparkler," recalled Goble. Mary Matthews was "reserved." Both helped women in immeasurable ways by using their natural talents, intelligence, and connections, often quietly working toward their goals while smiling in the faces of the men who tried to stand in their way. Dean Goble said, "Mary and Lella were shrewd women."

This is their story of opposite parallels.

Pivot Point

In every life, there is turning moment, a place on the axis of living that once a shift is made, one's future is changed. For Mary Matthews, that fault line came when she was seven years old and her mother lay dying.

In 1889, Hattie Beach Matthews was gravely ill. Her friend, Virginia Claypool Meredith, sat by her bedside. Hattie knew she was seriously ailing, and she worried about her seven-year-old daughter, Mary, and her two-year-old son, Meredith. Hattie had named her boy after Virginia as a tribute to their close friendship. The children's father had already passed away, and now Hattie lay on her deathbed. What would happen to her children after she was gone?

A childless widow who was making a name for herself as a "woman farmer," Virginia wanted to ease her friend's worries. She promised Hattie she would adopt her children if they were left orphans. Later that year, Hattie died and Virginia made good on her promise. Forty-year-old Virginia adopted Mary and Meredith. With that commitment, she became a single mother overnight and set Mary's course in motion.

Seven years earlier, around the time Mary Matthews was born in Peewee Valley, Kentucky, on October 13, 1882, Virginia had experienced her own monumental life shift. Her husband died and she chose to run their 115-acre ranch with prize shorthorn cattle and sheep. Virginia's unusual life as a farm manager and her belief that a woman could do anything, which had been instilled by her father, would subsequently influence the life of her newly adopted daughter.

⟨━━⟩

Virginia Claypool Meredith was born on Maplewood Farm near Connersville, Indiana, on November 5, 1848. She was the firstborn of the prosperous Austin and Hannah Claypool, who were progressive for their time. Austin believed his daughters should be given all of the advantages and educational opportunities his sons would receive. Virginia accompanied her father on horse and wagon rides to his pastures and fields, listening to his ideas on successful farming and business practices. Her father entertained men of prominence in their home. Political leaders, businessmen, and agriculturists were guests, and Virginia helped her mother as hostess when these men came to call. Virginia became accustomed to being in the presence of men of importance and power.

When Virginia was fifteen, she entered Glendale Female College in Glendale, Ohio, near Cincinnati. It was a premier private school for women in the Midwest attended by students from wealthy families. She graduated with honors in 1866 with a Bachelor of Arts degree.

On April 28, 1870, Virginia married Henry Clay Meredith, the only living son of Civil War General Solomon Meredith. The Civil War had taken a toll on the Meredith family. Henry's two older brothers, Samuel and David, died from wounds they received on the battlefield. Henry was the surviving brother who had served on his father's staff as a second lieutenant and *aide-de-camp*.

Virginia and Henry moved into Solomon Meredith's home, the famous Oakland Farm near Cambridge City, Indiana. The Federal-style house still stands today at 211 Meredith Street. Solomon raised livestock on his farm, including renowned herds of shorthorn cattle and flocks of Southdown sheep. When Virginia married Henry, the marriage connected two prominent, politically active agricultural families. Through her family experiences and education, Virginia was well prepared for her new role as wife and daughter-in-law in the influential Meredith family.

Virginia helped Henry's mother, Anna, manage the house, instruct the servants, and entertain guests, including politicians and stockbreeders who visited Oakland Farm. However, Virginia's work alongside Anna would be short-lived. Nineteen months after Virginia and Henry married, Anna died. The management of the Meredith home was left in the hands of twenty-three-year-old "Miss Virginia." Subsequently, Virginia became close to her father-in-law, Solomon, and she learned about raising purebred livestock, handling public sales, and establishing working relationships with the breeders who visited the farm. Little did she know then that the lessons she picked up from her father-in-law would one day serve her well.

Solomon died in 1875, leaving the management of the farm to Henry, who continued his father's tradition of entering and winning livestock shows and taking an active role in politics. He was elected to the Indiana General Assembly in 1881. As Henry became more active in politics, Virginia took on more of the day-to-day operations of Oakland Farm. She began to show and sell her own stock. Her new responsibilities turned out to be an apprenticeship for what was about to befall her.

Henry died of pneumonia at the age of thirty-eight on July 5, 1882, thrusting Virginia into the role of sole owner of Oakland Farm. At thirty-three, Virginia had a choice. She could return to her father's home or carry on the operations of the farm. She decided to manage her farm, a position that was unprecedented for a woman of that era. This was Virginia's juncture that would catapult her into national recognition as a respected agricultural speaker and writer. Four years after Henry's death, she would also become a single mother.

When she began to exhibit her livestock at the county and state fairs, Virginia was a conspicuous sight. A woman stockbreeder was unheard of, and sometimes her presence was met with disapproval and scorn. Yet she proved herself. Her animals competed well against the livestock bred and shown by men. She became a successful farm manager.

It was when she adopted Mary and Meredith Matthews that Virginia realized more fully the importance of home and child rearing. With two children to raise while managing a farm, Virginia formed a lifelong belief that running a home was equal to the work performed on a farm to make it fruitful and lucrative. This new chapter in Virginia's life forever spurred her to encourage home economics as a career for college-bound rural women. Mary Matthews would grow up to emulate the views and experiences of the remarkable woman who adopted her, the woman she called "Auntie."

⸙

Virginia became nationally known as a woman farmer who successfully ran her own crop production and livestock operation. Her financially successful farm opened doors to other opportunities. She spoke about livestock production to mostly male audiences. At the same time, Virginia was becoming a popular agricultural speaker; the education of the farming community was becoming a priority of the Indiana State Board of Agriculture. Both Virginia's father and her husband had served on this board.

Virginia was in the right place at the right time. The board decided to offer programs known as Farmers' Institutes. These meetings were the forerunner to those offered later by the Cooperative Extension Service, which would one day employ Mary Matthews and Lella Gaddis.

Farmers' Institutes gave farmers opportunities to learn about the latest developments in agriculture. The Indiana General Assembly passed the Farmers' Institute Act of 1889, which gave management of the program to Purdue University. Professor of Agriculture William C. Latta managed the program. Latta strongly believed that Purdue should offer women opportunities to better themselves by obtaining an education. He included topics of importance to women and utilized women speakers, such as Virginia, at the Farmers' Institutes.

Virginia is considered the first woman to be hired by Purdue's Agricultural Extension Department. The Institutes launched Virginia's career as a speaker and writer. Virginia was a devoted speaker for nearly twenty years and became Latta's close colleague. As a youngster, Mary tagged along, watching her mother's successes and meeting important people along the way.

⸙

The World's Columbian Exposition, known as the Chicago World's Fair, was hosted by the United States in 1893 to commemorate the 400th anniversary of Christopher Columbus's first voyage to the New World. The fair proved to be a life-changing catalyst for Virginia and for American women.

In 1890 (a year after Virginia adopted Mary and Meredith), President Benjamin Harrison signed the World's Fair Bill that named Chicago as the location for the exposition. The World's Columbian Commission, which was comprised of 108 male commissioners, was established to work with organizers from Chicago to turn 586 acres of swampland into Chicago's "White City" where the world's best inventors, artists, writers, and manufacturers displayed their talents.

Initially thought to be of little importance by the men, an amendment to the World's Fair Bill gave women a voice and brought them national attention. It also provided Virginia with an opportunity to advance her work for women. Illinois Representative William Springer was responsible for an amendment that required the appointment of a "Board of Lady Managers." This women's board would determine how contributions by women would be managed at the exposition. Female judges were to be assigned to bestow awards to exhibits created by women.

Each state was to have four women represented on the Board of Lady Managers. Judge Elijah B. Martindale, an Indiana Republican on the commission, recommended Virginia to become one of the lady managers from his state. Martindale and Virginia were longtime friends who knew one another from their affiliation with the Indiana Shorthorn Breeders' Association.

Bertha Palmer was president of the board, and Virginia was named vice chair. Bertha was the wife of Potter Palmer. Potter loved his wife so much, he gave her a lavish hotel, The Palmer House of Chicago, as a wedding gift. Virginia was one of Bertha's circle of advisors, dubbed the "favored few." Bertha gave Virginia the assignment of working with foreign dignitaries, lobbying Congress, soothing egos, launching projects, and writing reports. In 1892, Bertha rewarded Virginia's dedication by appointing her chair of the Board of Lady Managers Committee on Awards. Her work with the World's Columbian Exposition garnered Virginia and other lady managers celebrity status that followed them throughout their lives. She was often introduced as the "lady manager from Indiana."

While the Board of Lady Managers met with numerous challenges posed by men on the World's Columbian Commission (due to their prejudices against females), these determined women played a major role in the six-month World's Columbian Exposition. They had their own building and administrators at a time when women were striving for more rights. For the first time, women's creative and intellectual works were recognized and displayed in an international setting. The World's Columbian Exposition gave Virginia a countrywide platform. Her reputation blossomed beyond Cambridge City and Indiana to burst forth into national prominence.

Virginia was active with the Chicago World's Fair from 1890 through 1894. Where were her newly adopted children when she was in Chicago? There is no record of Mary and Meredith accompanying Virginia to the World's Columbian Exposition or of a nanny or relative tending to their care. More than likely, the sister and brother paid a visit or two to the historic venue. How Virginia juggled motherhood and her position on the Board of Lady Managers is a story that women today would be eager to hear, yet it is left to our imaginations.

In 1895, after her entrance into the national spotlight with the World's Columbian Exposition, Virginia, age forty-seven, joined governors and other dignitaries to speak at the Inter-State Agricultural Institute at Vicksburg, Mississippi. It was a grand affair with 250 people waiting on the platform as a special train car brought the prominent guests to the Vicksburg depot.

The theme of the conference was "How could a profit be turned from farming?" Her speech, "Profitable Sheep Husbandry," was record breaking. Up until this time in the South, it was considered inappropriate for a woman to speak in public. Virginia's speech captivated the audience, and during the final evening ceremonies, she was presented with a gold medal inscribed with words deeming her "the Queen of American Agriculture." The woman who thirteen years earlier made the unconventional choice to manage a farm was stunned.

In 1897, Virginia went to the University of Minnesota to become the preceptress of the School of Agriculture and start a home economics program. Fifteen-year-old Mary and ten-year-old Meredith followed their mother there to live in a new women's dormitory that was more like a large, finely furnished home. An elaborately built facility, it housed 120 girls who were under Virginia's watch. In Minneapolis, Mary attended high school and later the university. Mary was the first woman to earn a bachelor's degree in home economics from the University of Minnesota in 1904.

Not much is known about Mary's brother, Meredith. It is believed he was born in Indianapolis, Indiana, on September 29, 1887. When Virginia left the University of Minnesota in 1903 to return to full-time farming in Cambridge City, Mary stayed behind to finish her degree. However, Meredith moved back to Oakland Farms with his mother to attend Central High School. He graduated in 1906. The next year, he attended Purdue University. Eventually, he worked as an engineer and spent most of his adult life living in California.

It appears Meredith was not as close to his mother as his sister. Perhaps the lack of a father figure caused him to separate himself from the females in his family. Whatever the psychological reasoning, it seems Meredith was not a big part of the lives of Virginia and Mary, who shared their work and home life until Virginia's death in 1936. The two women had much in common, and perhaps their verve for agriculture, home economics, and women's advancement left the boy who bore his adoptive mother's surname to find his own way.

❧

Virginia enjoyed her time at the University of Minnesota until 1902, when she and the new principal of the School of Agriculture, Frederick D. Tucker, locked heads over who was in charge of the women students. Virginia insisted that she had jurisdiction over the women; Principal Tucker claimed that he had authority over the girls and the boys. Tucker brought the matter to the University of Minnesota Board of Regents. By the time the board heard the complaint, it was spring of 1903, and Virginia had completed her term and returned to Indiana.

After their investigation, the board called for the resignations of both Tucker and Virginia. Newspaper reports claimed that Virginia had overstepped her authority, making Tucker uncomfortable in fulfilling his duties. Both parties resigned.

Meanwhile, Professor Latta had been attempting to parlay the interests of women at the Farmers' Institutes into support for the implementation of home economics courses at Purdue University. In 1897 during the Winter Short Courses at Purdue, he provided programs for women with Virginia as speaker, but few attended. Because of the low enrollment, Purdue President Winthrop Stone was apprehensive about creating a Department of Household Economics. Latta also held a Women's Conference in 1901 with more than two dozen women invited to hear Virginia as the keynote speaker. Still, he had little support for a home economics program.

After she left the University of Minnesota, Virginia resumed her presentations at the Farmers' Institutes to help Latta in his effort to garner backing. She also used her former position as a university professor to lobby President Stone. Virginia wanted not only a home economics program at Purdue, but also equal representation for women in agriculture courses.

～♦♦～

Latta's efforts to establish home economics courses at Purdue took place at the time of the historic Lake Placid Conferences. Home economics grew out of a series of annual conferences held between 1899 and 1909. The first conference was held at Mr. and Mrs. Melville Dewey's retreat nestled in the peaceful forest of New York's Adirondack Mountains. Those who attended included Ellen Swallow Richards, the founder of "home economics"—a term created at the conference. (She originally wanted to call the discipline "oekology," the science of right living, or "euthenics," the science of controllable environment.)

At the turn of the century, bacteria had just been discovered, and people were eager to examine everything under a microscope. Those who attended the first Lake Placid Conference arrived to begin a study of home sanitation, and they were interested in developing a body of knowledge for new domestic science departments forming at colleges. The attendees believed that home economics was to be a distinct section of economics and that it should be a college course of study, not to be confused with "household arts" (e.g., dusting, cleaning, and mending). They also discussed the preparation of women for leadership in this new field. The founders acknowledged early on that an educational and scientific association was necessary to formalize the profession of home economics.

The culmination of these conferences was the formation of the American Home Economics Association (AHEA), founded in 1909.

This was a national "umbrella" organization for home economics subgroups that would be started in each state.

With its scenic mountain views, gushing waterfalls, and natural allure, Lake Placid was the perfect setting for a gathering of like minds to give rise to a discipline that would benefit women and their families for generations.

With thoughts of Lake Placid surely in their psyches, Professor Latta and Virginia continued to pursue the creation of a home economics department at Purdue University.

Rossville Roots

A photo taken in 1902 of Lella Reed Gaddis, age twenty-five, captures the strength and energy of the woman who was a "go-getter." In the monochrome snapshot, Lella is pictured with her three siblings, Mary "Mamie," Bertha "Kate," and John "Clyde." A fourth sister died in infancy. Also in the photograph is her brother-in-law, Henry Clay Riley, a Methodist minister, sister-in-law, Sally Henderson, and her nephew, Paul, age eight, the apple of Lella's eye. Paul was the only child of Mamie and Henry.

The handsomely dressed group is at a park in Indiana. They stand shoulder to shoulder in a "trench" with a stone opening at one end. Perhaps the channel is a storm drain. The photo is a curious sight with the family dressed to the nines, peering chest deep from a furrow.

It must be a summer day; nephew Paul's feet are bare. The women are dressed in crisp white. Their shirts and blouses have "detachable" collars that were popular fashion at the turn of the century. The women have their hair pinned atop their heads. Lella looks at the photographer, head on, shoulders back, while others in her family lean ever so slightly, waiting for the "Brownie" to click.

Lella's high cheekbones and slight smile give her a regal air, and her erect posture is reminiscent of a self-assured Victorian woman. It is evident that the horseback riding lessons she took from her brother

In 1902, the Gaddis children and their spouses, along with Mamie and Henry's son Paul, pose at a park in Indiana. Left: Paul Gaddis Riley, Sally Henderson Gaddis, Mary M. "Mamie" Gaddis Riley, Henry Clay Riley, Bertha Kate Gaddis, Lella Reed Gaddis, and John Clyde Gaddis. Courtesy of Miriam Epple-Heath.

have engraved the physical memory of her excellent carriage. To Lella's right is her sister Kate, age thirty-four, a schoolteacher. Kate leans on her elbow with her hand at her cheek, partially covering her face. The sisters are opposites, even in stance.

Neither Lella nor Kate married; they were working women, after all. It was common practice and accepted that once a woman married, her employer would terminate her. Until Kate's death in 1947, the sisters lived together, pooling their money. Kate was sickly and a homebody who loved the "little dears" she taught. Lella rarely had a headache and later traveled back roads, highways, and rail corridors teaching rural women throughout Indiana. The Gaddis sisters were complementary contrasts.

Lella Reed Gaddis was born to William Alfred and Margaret Elizabeth Reed Gaddis on May 29, 1877. She was the youngest of four surviving children born to a prominent pioneer family who purchased their farm in Rossville, Indiana, from the government.

In 1862 at the age of twenty-two, William enlisted for three-years in the 77th Indiana Regiment, 4th Calvary in the Civil War. On September 13, 1863, he became a prisoner of war. Initially, William was sent to Richmond, Virginia. However, the large number of Federal prisoners there prompted Confederate officials to build a place of greater security at Andersonville, Georgia, or Camp Sumter (not to be confused with Fort Sumter, in Charleston Harbor, South Carolina, where the shots initiating the Civil War were fired). William was transferred to Andersonville in 1864.

Andersonville Civil War Prison was built as a "stockade for Union enlisted men." It was notorious for its overcrowding, starvation, disease, and cruelty. The prison sat on twenty-seven acres and was enclosed by a high wall made of pine logs. Originally intended to hold ten thousand men, Camp Sumter heaved with thirty-three thousand. The death rate at Andersonville was the highest of all Civil War prisons.

While Lella's father was a prisoner at Camp Sumter, he experienced and witnessed evils of heart and mind. According to diaries kept by prisoners, the men were desperate for food and resorted to cooking and eating dogs. They contended with head lice. Dishes and eating utensils were scarce, so men used old shoes and dirty caps for the molasses or thin soup they would receive. To stay warm, they robbed the dead of their clothing. Each morning at nine, a lone drummer appeared at the south gate and steadily beat, summoning the camp to deliver the dead.

After eight months at Andersonville, William was paroled to Charleston, South Carolina. He was "mustered out" on July 19, 1865. William traveled home by troop train. When he was dropped off in Rossville, William walked across the fields toward his home. His family saw him approaching but did not recognize him. He weighed eighty pounds.

❧

On March 7, 1866, William married Margaret Elizabeth Reed. Their first child, Mary Maria "Mamie," was born exactly nine months later, to the day, on December 7. In two-year stair steps, Bertha Kate and

John Clyde arrived. Lella Reed was a postscript, born seven years after her only brother.

When Lella was a child, her family moved from Rossville to a farm on Cason Road north of West Lafayette, Indiana. She attended a one-room country school. In the fall of 1888, Lella's sister Kate began her teaching career at Lafayette's Columbian School at the southeast corner of Owen and Highland Streets, close to where the family would later move. Highland School would be built on this site in 1923.

When Lella was fourteen, her father was elected sheriff of Tippecanoe County. The family moved to the apartment above the county jail that was provided for the sheriff at Fourth and Alabama Streets in Lafayette. (Today the site is a parking lot for jurors of the Tippecanoe County Courts.) Lella attended Lafayette High School, where classmates sometimes teased her about living in a jail. Interesting that William, a prisoner of war, made his home in a jail. Perhaps his cruel incarceration at Andersonville made him a more compassionate sheriff to his prisoners. During this time, Mamie married Reverend Henry Clay Riley in a wedding ceremony held in the jail's residence. Lella, sixteen, acted as usher at the nuptials. Their mother Margaret gave the couple a long, white, linen damask tablecloth as a wedding gift.

When William's term as sheriff ended in 1894, the Gaddis family moved to a home at Fifth and Central Streets in the Highland Park neighborhood. The Highland Park Land Company—whose stockholders included the father and uncles of David E. Ross, who would become a renowned Purdue benefactor—had developed this former pastureland a few years earlier. Lella graduated from Lafayette High School in 1896. At that time, her father was the treasurer for the Hamilton Furniture and Carpet Company in Lafayette.

Lella's mother Margaret passed away in 1900. Two years later, the photo was taken of the Gaddis siblings, their spouses, and little Paul standing in the "trench" in their best bib and tucker. They are motherless, adult children in this turn-of-the-century summer moment captured for eternity.

❦

In 1906, William lived with his two daughters, Lella, 29, and Kate, 38, at 310 North Salisbury. This was the year Kate began writing in her leather-bound line-a-day diaries. Every day for forty years she faithfully

Kate, sister of Lella Reed Gaddis, wrote in her line-a-day diaries from 1906 until 1946, record-ing snippets of her days, from hanging the wash on the line and killing a hen for dinner to hearing of the sinking of the Titanic. Photograph by Jack Klink.

jotted down a few lines about her life. These palm-sized journals con-tain sparse recordings of both mundane tasks and monumental mo-ments. She wrote of the small nuances such as hanging clothes in the yard to dry or killing a hen for dinner, to the larger-than-life events such as Booker T. Washington speaking at Purdue and the sinking of the Titanic. Each 365-day span was given its due in a rich, cranberry-hued book turned historic gem with the year engraved upon the cover.

By this time, Kate was teaching at Washington School on Elizabeth Street in Lafayette. From Kate's diary it appears that Lella was already connected with Purdue and some of the "movers and shakers" of the University. Lella helped care for the new baby of her friends, Mr. and Mrs. John H. Skinner. At the time, Skinner was professor of animal husbandry. Later, he was promoted to dean of the School of Agricul-ture, succeeding Professor Latta, who was never officially named dean. Eventually, Skinner was responsible for teaching agriculture courses, managing faculty, and operating the Purdue University Farm and Creamery.

On Sunday, January 21, 1906, Kate writes in her diary, "Very rainy. Home all day. Finished reading 'Nedra.' Heard the 'Little Skinner' arrived the night before in the rain and wind."

Published in 1905, Nedra is a novel by George Barr McCutcheon, a popular novelist and playwright. George was from Tippecanoe County, Indiana. He attended Purdue and roomed with George Ade, the famous humorist who developed a lifelong friendship with George McCutcheon's brother, noted cartoonist, John T. McCutcheon, who is known as the "Dean of American Cartoonists." In 1890, the two friends worked together at the Chicago Morning News, later known as the Chicago Record. George Ade wrote the column Stories of the Streets and the Town, which John McCutcheon illustrated. In 1903, John McCutcheon joined the staff of the Chicago Tribune where he worked until his retirement in 1946. He was awarded the Pulitzer Prize for Editorial Cartooning in 1932. Purdue's McCutcheon Hall is named for the famous cartoonist.

George Ade was a tireless fund-raiser for Purdue. He and David Ross purchased and donated the Tilt Farm to Purdue in 1922 for the site of what would become Ross-Ade Stadium.

In 1908, Ade's musical comedy, The Fair Co-Ed, was produced by Purdue's Harlequin Club before it went to Broadway. Perhaps this play is what Kate refers to in her entry from September 23, 1908: "George Ade entertains most of Purdue."

Kate was a member of a literature class, and throughout her diaries she recorded the books she read that touched on issues of the time or related to current trends. On February 28, 1908, she writes, "Went to the Literature Class. We do have such a nice time. Am studying 'A Doll's House.'"

A Doll's House was an 1879 play by Norwegian playwright Henrik Ibsen. In its heyday, the play created a sensation and is now his most famous play. A Doll's House is often termed the first true feminist play. It was controversial when first published because it criticizes the norms of marriage in the nineteenth century. At one time, A Doll's House was required reading in secondary schools and universities. Kate was a bookish schoolteacher and homebody, who read the current, notorious novels of her day.

Kate's Literature Class studied a trio of work by Henrik Ibsen in 1908. She mentions reading two more plays, Ghosts and An Enemy of *the People. Ghosts* is "a family drama in three acts" written in 1881. Like *A Doll's House, Ghosts* was considered scandalous by many of the era because Ibsen challenged the moralities and family values of the Victorian time, and the play was deemed indecent for its veiled references to syphilis. She writes on April 13, 1908, "Went to the Literature Class. We finished 'Ghosts.' Had such a nice time."

Ibsen wrote *An Enemy of the People* in 1882 in response to the public outcry against *Ghosts. An Enemy of the People* addresses the irrational tendencies of the masses, and the hypocritical and corrupt nature of the political system that they support. It is the story of one brave man's struggle to do the right thing and speak the truth in the face of extreme social intolerance.

❧

Kate mentioned many of the boarders she and Lella had in their home. Most were Purdue students who rented a room, sometimes in exchange for chores around the house. Throughout their lives, they would supplement their incomes by taking in boarders, renting to Purdue faculty and building new homes to rent and reside. Comments about money and bills are scattered through the diaries. It sounds as if their father had some financial difficulties.

> November 9, 1907: Pa did not pay the grocery bill. We had to.

> January 26, 1908: Pay day. Draw pay and pay debts. Having only a pleasant smile left. Teeth fixed $3.00.

> April 22, 1908: Pay day. All in. All out.

Boarders would come and go with the courses offered at Purdue. On Wednesday, January 10, 1906, Kate writes, "Corn School on." In the early 1900s, the idea of a corn club was established for boys in public schools. The Farmers' Institutes were behind the movement to organize boys and girls clubs, holding institutes for youth. Girls had what was sometimes referred to as "Tomato Clubs" or "Canning Clubs," where they had contests in home gardening and vegetable preserving.

Lella, age twenty-five, and Kate, age thirty-four, pose with their beloved nephew Paul Gaddis Riley, age eight, in 1902. Paul roomed in his aunts' home when he attended Purdue University. During World War I, Paul was a member of an elite group of Army pilots assigned to the Liberty Bond campaign. He flew a Curtis J4 "Jenny" aircraft, performing acrobatic stunts to draw crowds and promote the purchase of Liberty Bonds. Courtesy of Miriam Epple-Heath.

These clubs were the precursor to 4-H and were significant in the development of the Cooperative Extension Service.

Boys were given grains of corn and then instructed by an experienced corn grower on how to prepare the soil, plant, and care for the vegetable. A contest was held for the best corn with premiums given such as a garden plow, a buggy whip, or money. Part of the curriculum included an "excursion" to Purdue. From the diaries, it looks as if the young men who came to Purdue for "Corn School" needed overnight accommodations, and Lella and Kate rented out their spare bedrooms. Kate also talked of Chautauqua.

Chautauqua was a very popular adult education summer camp movement in the United States in the late nineteenth and early twentieth centuries. It began at Lake Chautauqua, New York, in 1874, with a ten-day program presented by Sunday school teachers that combined instruction, recreation, and entertainment. Chautauqua assemblies expanded and spread throughout rural America until the mid-1920s. It brought entertainment and culture to a community with speakers, teachers, musicians, entertainers, preachers, and specialists of the day. William Jennings Bryan, a Prohibitionist who ran for president three times and lost, spoke with his populist and evangelical message on topics such as temperance. He was the most popular Chautauqua speaker until his death in 1925.

Chautauquas and Farmers' Institutes brought social enrichment and education to rural Americans who were thirsty for connection and knowledge. When radio and "picture shows" came on the scene, the Chautauqua experienced entertainment competition, and they began to decline in popularity.

In her diaries, Kate referred to the Farmers' Institute program that coincided with Chautauqua. More than likely, Kate and Lella heard

Virginia Meredith speak at Chautauquas and Farmers' Institutes. Lecture topics for these educational and social gatherings pertained to the farm, home, and family and spoke profoundly of issues of the time. Yet some topics could even relate to current struggles and interests. Lecture titles included:

- Care of Cream and Churning

- The Hessian Fly

- Our Daughters—What Shall We Teach Them?

- The Value of Higher Education for the Farmer

- Sanitation of the Farmer's Home

- Fruit Growing and Spraying

- Mothers on the Farm

- Needs and Improvements of Our Rural Schools

The first time Mary Matthews was mentioned in Kate's diaries is on November 15, 1907: "Am making aprons for the church fair. Lella called on Miss Matthews."

Throughout her diaries, Kate tells of who "called." She means, of course, who came to visit. The journals give a perspective on the sisters' social life. Lella and Kate often visited friends and relatives, staying for lunch, dinner, or overnight at the spur of the moment. In turn, friends and relatives came to their home for meals. Lella and Kate attended parties, teas, socials, weddings, "stork parties" (what are now called baby showers), and Purdue lectures. Kate tended to stay home more, often nursing a stomachache or sore feet. Lella attended faculty dances and picnics at Columbian Park. She went canoeing, horseback riding, and camping. From Dean Skinner to George Ade, Grover Cleveland to Theodore Roosevelt, the names Kate drops are like a "Who's Who" of Tippecanoe County, Purdue University, and the nation in the early part of the twentieth century:

February 15, 1907: Lella went to Stones for a party [Winthrop E. Stone, president of Purdue University, 1900 to 1921].

August 21, 1907, [Chautauqua in session]: Buffalo Bill here today. Mamie, Henry, Paul, Lella and myself attend.

January 19, 1908: Miss Matthews and Miss Spitzer called in the afternoon. Such a beautiful day. Just like spring.

October 20, 1908: Bryan here. [President-elect William Jennings Bryan] West side school out to hear him. But we just teach school and say nothing.

October 23, 1908: Pa attends Taft Day all day. Lella sees and hears Taft [President-elect William Howard Taft].

It is unusual for both Bryan and Taft to visit Lafayette within three days of each other as they campaigned for the 1908 presidential election. Taft was known as a stay-at-home candidate, riding on the coattails of Theodore Roosevelt, who supported Taft, his Secretary of War. Taft's campaigning was kept to a minimum, with all posters and postcards of Taft containing either a reference to or picture of Roosevelt.

On the other side of the fence, Bryan fought to prove he would be better suited to follow Roosevelt. His campaign managers coined the acronym "TAFT—Takes Advice from Theodore." Bryan invented the national "stumping tour," where he gave speeches across the country (seemingly because he stood on tree stumps to speak to crowds). Bryan made a huge blunder in late August, calling for the federal government to take over the running of the railroads. Such socialist leanings were sacrilege, and this statement cost him the election.

Kate sounded miffed that her principal and school ignored the fact that William Jennings Bryan visited the community. His "railroad blunder" in August may have been the reason why her school chose not to acknowledge Bryan's presence in Lafayette. More than likely, Kate wished she could have tagged along with Lella and their father to see history in the making and hear Taft's speech. Of course, these bright, aware women did not yet have the right to vote.

On November 15, 1908, Kate writes, "Called on Mrs. Christie and were at Mrs. Skinner's for tea."

It is interesting that Kate would mention visits to both Mrs. Christie and Mrs. Skinner on the same day, in the same sentence. Mrs. Christie's husband, George I. Christie, became director of the Department of Agricultural Extension and all of the associated field agents. He was also the director of the Agricultural Experiment Station.

John Skinner and George Christie were strong-willed men who eventually locked horns. In the book the *Queen of American Agriculture*, authors Frederick Whitford, Andrew G. Martin, and Phyllis Mattheis write of President Edward Elliott's frustrations with the two men in the late 1920s: "Elliott was tired of what he thought was too much duplication of programs, too much infighting among the agriculture faculty, and too little cooperation between the three main agricultural programs: teaching, research, and extension. . . . President Elliott felt that these men did little in the way of working cooperatively" (p. 261).

Early on, Lella and Kate were connected to the influential men in Purdue's Agricultural Department. Lella's bond with the Skinners and her association with the Christies may have had a strong bearing on why the "Ag Boys" wanted Lella in their department when she became the first state leader of home demonstration.

It is obvious from Kate's records that she enjoyed puttering around the house, and she did not like change:

> February 15, 1908: Have such a nice time doing as I please. [She wrote this statement often throughout all of her diaries, particularly when Lella was away.]

> March 25: Had a call from Mr. Kendle of the Indianapolis Schools. Am invited to teach for him at $700 per year. Scared most out of my wits.

In 1908, Lella may have had a suitor who left the country but kept in contact. Kate scrawled notes about Lella visiting friends and attending a party with Mr. M. Kelley. Then on June 26, Kate writes, "Mr. Kelley goes to Honolulu in the morning." She follows this entry on June 27, "Get awake at 4 o'clock in time to hear the Big 4 train steam off with Mr. Kelley to Honolulu."

The passenger train to which Kate referred would have departed from the Big Four Train Depot near the Wabash River in downtown Lafayette. The train would take Mr. Kelley to the West coast where he would board a ship and travel to Honolulu, Hawaii—a very long trip at the turn of the century.

Throughout the remainder of the year and into the next, Kate wrote that Lella received letters from Mr. Kelley while he was in Hawaii. It is interesting to ponder the reasoning behind which events of the day Kate chose to note for posterity in her diaries. Did she pen the first thing that popped into her head as she sat down to write? Or did she sit and think over her day, gleaning the jewels, extracting the thorns, recording the common slices of living for a future time to behold? On December 23, 1909, she writes, "Lella gets a package from Honolulu—purple house jacket in it."

Kate deemed the Honolulu letters and package important fodder for her diary. Was she intrigued with her little sister's relationship with Mr. Kelley? Was she slightly envious when the Christmas parcel arrived and such a personal gift as a house jacket was tucked inside? One can see Lella with her model-like posture slipping her arms into the coat, intended for wear at home, as sister Kate looked on. Later, Kate would sit with her pocket journal and record the day.

It's Science

In 1904, Virginia Meredith spoke to the all-male Indiana State Board of Agriculture about Purdue's need to establish a home economics course. The men in their day coats and stiff-collared shirts held their felt hats and gazed at this candid woman farmer. For men and women, Virginia was a curiosity of the time. Her speech was very progressive regarding women and their roles. It took courage and assurance to speak as she did that day:

> I think there is a special need for the training of women to be farmers. . . . it has come to pass that girls inherit farms. Sometimes they do not know what to do with them. There are a great many women who never get married for the very best of reasons. May be you don't know what they are. There are not enough good men to go around. . . . there is no business to my mind so suitable to women as farming . . . . I see there is need for special training. If we are trained in an agricultural school by a professor who understands what he is doing, we will get the science, art and philosophy, and we will be equipped to live.

After years of stalling the efforts of Professor William Latta and Virginia Meredith to start a home economics program at Purdue, President Winthrop Stone finally reconsidered. Together with members of the Purdue University Board of Trustees, he created a Department of Household Economics within the School of Science in the fall of 1905.

Virginia Claypool Meredith was courageously progressive in her personal and professional life. In 1882, her husband died unexpectedly, and at thirty-three, she decided to manage their 115-acre southern Indiana farm. Seven years later, she adopted two children, becoming a single mother overnight. One of those children was Mary L. Matthews. Virginia would go on to become the first woman on the Purdue University Board of Trustees. Courtesy of Purdue University Libraries, Archives and Special Collections.

Conceivably, Stone experienced political pressure to institute a home economics course. By this time, many of the land-grant universities had followed the recommendations of the Lake Placid Conferences and had already established departments of home economics. Other Midwest colleges formed a School of Domestic Science positioned in the School of Agriculture. Stone did not go that far, yet he expressed these sentiments: "Purdue should offer to women opportunities comparable in scientific and technical value with those enjoyed by men."

Purdue historians William Murray Hepburn, former librarian, and Louis Martin Sears, former professor of History, wrote, among other books, *Purdue University: Fifty Years of Progress.* They put Stone's delayed response to the Lake Placid proposal in perspective with these blunt remarks, "The action of Purdue in 1905 was considerably belated. The University deserves no credit as a pioneer."

Perhaps Purdue, in general, does not deserve credit as a pioneer with regard to a course in home economics, but the women who first stepped on campus to teach and develop the department certainly warrant acclaim.

Ivy Frances Harner was hired to head the new Department of Household Economics. She was a home economics teacher from Kansas State Agricultural College. After earning a B.S. and M.S. from Kansas State, she studied domestic science in Europe from 1904 to 1905. Harner had just completed her studies overseas before arriving at Purdue in horse and carriage. It would be four more years before Henry Ford made his first Model T and several more years before automobiles would be seen motoring around campus. More than likely, Harner wore a straight-front corset under her long dress, making her waist as small as possible, as was the fashion of the time. Upon arrival, she would have stepped off her carriage onto Purdue soil in high-buttoned shoes.

Harner's office and classrooms were in Ladies Hall, which was not in the best of conditions. Built in 1872 as a boarding house, Ladies Hall was the first permanent Purdue building to be erected north of State Street. When Purdue opened in September 1874, Ladies Hall housed the college dining hall, living quarters for new faculty and their families, and the office for Purdue's first president, Abraham C. Shortridge.

For a time, the building was also known as Art Hall because art classes were taught there on the first floor. Yet during most of its existence, Ladies Hall was used as the women's dormitory. Instructors lived there, too. It faced State Street and was where Stone Hall stands today. When Harner began her tenure, Ladies Hall was a shabby building with rough wooden floors and roll top desks. There was a laboratory with desks for sixteen students. All students living on campus were served twenty-one meals each week in the dining hall at a total cost of $2.50. A plump, smiling woman named Mrs. Stockton presided over the refectory.

A suite of rooms was available for the home economics students. Girls received male guests in the "reception parlor." In the 1919 *Debris* yearbook, an essay entitled "Memories of the 'Hall'" describes the parlor located in the "upper or celestial region" as being sparsely furnished but "it made no difference. Eliminating all possibilities of handholding, that old parlor was a sort of oasis in the desert of college routine." Emma Mont McRae was the chaperone for the residential area, and she was affectionately referred to as "Mother McRae." The essay said, "The Ladies' Hall! A Temple dedicated to Romance and Art and Food! No wonder we loved it and feel constrained to give it this heartfelt obituary."

As early as 1913, girls were longing for a new building. In the *Debris* of that year it states, "The laboratory space as it now exists is entirely inadequate for the number of girls enrolled in the course. However, those who are leaving hope to return in a few years to see a new Women's Building with well-equipped laboratories and ample room for all those who are interested in Home Economics." It would be 1922 before a new building would be erected, known today as Matthews Hall. Ladies Hall was demolished in 1927, making it one of the first major university buildings to disappear from campus.

The 1907 *Debris* describes the early Department of Household Economics as providing "economical and scientific study of such subjects as food principles . . . classification of food, chemical and microscopic composition of food, application of heat to food principles, economical and nutritive value of foods . . . food preservation and adulteration and dietetics." The courses were not about baking cookies and learning laundry skills. From the beginning, they were about the science of foods, the chemistry that makes them nutritious, and the preservation necessary to hold the nutritional value.

Clinical nutrition is the study of the relationship between food and a healthy body. More specifically, it is the science of nutrients and how they are digested, absorbed, transported, metabolized, stored, and eliminated from the body. Clinical nutrition was new when Harner came to Purdue to organize the first home economics courses. It was first developed in the early 1900s, when scientists discovered that some diseases, such as beriberi, scurvy, rickets, and pellagra seemed to be caused by diets that lacked certain foods.

Harner resigned in 1908 and went on to serve as head of the Domestic Science Department of the Louisiana Industrial Institute. Henrietta W. Calvin, also from Kansas State Agricultural College, assumed the direction of Purdue's Home Economics Department. Calvin had an impressive background in academics and family life. She graduated from Kansas State in 1886 and a week later married her husband,

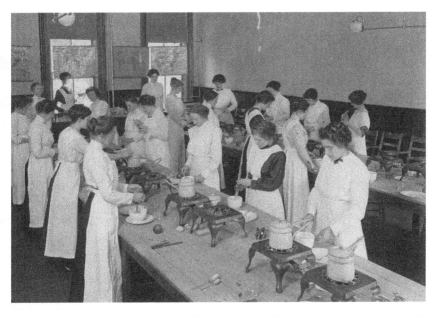

Women take a home economics cookery class in Ladies Hall at Purdue University in the early 1900s. The 1907 Debris yearbook describes the early home economics department as providing "economical and scientific study of such subjects as food principles . . . classification of food, chemical and microscopic composition of food, application of heat to food principles, economical and nutritive value of foods . . . food preservation and adulteration and dietetics." Courtesy of Purdue University Libraries, Archives and Special Collections.

John. She was a homemaker for eleven years raising her five children while continuing to educate herself by reading about law, political science, home nursing, pediatrics, and dietetics. After her husband died in 1898, she became a librarian and domestic science professor at her alma mater. When Calvin came to Purdue to head the Home Economics Department, she was a widow raising five children. She served at Purdue for four years before she moved on to become dean of home economics for Oregon State University.

In 1900, Mary Matthews graduated from the St. Anthony School of Agriculture where she had enrolled after arriving in Minnesota with her mother. She continued her education at Minnesota's land-grant college, the University of Minnesota. When Mary was awarded her diploma at the 1904 commencement exercises, she received more applause than did any other graduate in the class. The reason for the bounteous applause was that Mary was the first women to receive a degree of Bachelor of Science in home economics from the University of Minnesota. This was the same year that Virginia Meredith presented her courageous speech to the State Board of Agriculture, advocating education for women. Ironically, at the time that Virginia's daughter graduated from the University of Minnesota, Purdue did not offer even one course in home economics.

After graduation, Mary returned to her mother's farm in Cambridge City for a couple of years before moving to Lafayette in 1907 to teach clothing (construction and care) in the Lafayette Industrial School at Seventh and Columbia Streets in Lafayette. The Industrial School was part of the Lafayette Free Kindergarten and Industrial School Association. The Industrial School was for girls ages eight through sixteen and offered instruction in sewing, cooking, music, literature, and needlecrafts. The school closed in 1916. Both the Industrial School and the kindergarten were "replaced" by the public school system. Mary taught there for one year, and then returned to the University of Minnesota where she taught clothing for another year.

Mary and the Gaddis sisters moved in the same circles on and off campus as is evident with Kate's mention of the Industrial School in her diary: "January 21, 1910: I went to the Industrial School for a teachers meeting then on down to the doctors."

Across State Street on the Purdue campus, the School of Agriculture was evolving as well. In 1906, it organized its outreach effort of Farmers' Institutes as "Extension Work" within the Agricultural Experiment Station. Highly regarded for his work in this area, George I. Christie was named director. He was Canadian and a graduate of Ontario Agricultural College in Guelph, Ontario. Christie was said to never have given a talk, but always a speech, and the timbre of his voice reached the farthest listener in the largest crowd. In those days, speakers used megaphones when talking to large groups, but Christie did not need one. In his derby hat, he was said to be "the preacher of the gospel of the science of agriculture."

Mary Matthews had become acquainted with Christie while working with her mother at Farmers' Institutes. Christie hired Mary as an instructor in home economics extension within the School of Agriculture. In 1910 at the age of twenty-eight, Mary, tall and raven-haired, arrived on the Purdue campus to join the faculty. Her Purdue future was but a narrow footpath then, but it would meander along a wide career trail parallel to a rewarding personal road of club memberships and service. She would live in West Lafayette for her entire life, build a school from scratch, and make Purdue and the betterment of women her life's work.

Yet later, it would be Lella and Kate Gaddis who would become very close friends with Christie, his wife, and children. They would eat in one another's homes, spend holidays together, and become like family. The Christie's names are peppered throughout Kate's diaries.

When Mary came to Purdue, there were about forty women students on campus. Mary made educating homemakers her sole aim and ambition. In the beginning, home economics extension work in Indiana was her baby. One of her initial tasks was to organize the household economics courses offered at Purdue's first summer school. Lella and Kate took a class that year organized by Miss Matthews.

1910 was also the year of Halley's Comet, which passes in the earth's orbit on average every seventy-six years. By Kate's notes, people thought the world might end, much like the talk leading up to the year 2000 with the predictions of Armageddon or a natural world disaster. She writes:

> May 18, 1910: Tonight is the time for the comet to take us off the earth. We "the earth" pass through its tail this evening from 9-11. We are going up to the Smiths to attend their "roof party."

> May 19, 1910: Here we are safe and sound. Halley's Comet did not hit us.

The earth passed through the end of the comet's tail for six hours on May 19. Despite some published reports leading up to the event, the comet's tail did not contain poisonous gases, and there was never any danger of a celestial collision. In anticipation of the comet's arrival, telescope sales skyrocketed and hotels in large cities offered special packages that included rooftop viewings. It appears Lella and Kate's friends, the Smiths, were quite in vogue with their "roof party" the night of Halley's grand show.

American author and humorist Mark Twain has an infamous connection to Halley's Comet. Twain was born in 1835 as the comet passed over. In 1909, knowing that Halley's Comet was due to make another pass the next year, Twain predicted that he would die when it came around again. Observatory telescopes picked up the comet on April 9, 1910, and followed it as it reached the point in its orbit when it was nearest to the sun on April 20. Twain died the next day. Kate juxtaposes the historical event with a mundane occurrence: "April 22: Mark Twain died last night. Ruth (good friend and fellow teacher) drags her mother down to the dentist and has her tooth out."

⁕

When Mary came to Purdue it was the Progressive Era in America, which lasted until World War I. Women were very influential in the Progressive Era and made many valuable changes in society. Although their most popular achievement was the passing of the 19th Amendment that gave all citizens the right to vote, they succeeded in much more. Some of their most successful accomplishments were development of settlement houses, the birth control movement, and the fight against alcohol.

During the 1910s, the number of labor unions grew. Unsafe working conditions were brought to the forefront by the horrific Triangle Shirtwaist Factory fire in New York City. The Triangle Shirtwaist Factory was on the eighth, ninth, and tenth floors of the Asch Building. The factory produced women's blouses, then known as "shirtwaists." The factory employed mostly immigrant girls between the ages of thirteen and twenty-three years of age who worked nine hours a day on weekdays plus seven hours on Saturdays. The company always kept its doors locked to ensure that the young girls stayed stooped over their sewing machines and did not "steal" anything. When a fire broke out on March 25, 1911, the locks sealed the fate of these helpless girls. In just thirty minutes, 146 perished.

Witnesses on the street thought the owners were tossing fabric out windows to save it and then realized girls in their ankle-length dresses were jumping. Some girls flung themselves down the elevator shaft in an attempt to escape.

The horror of the deaths of 146 teenage girls spurred a national crusade for workplace safety. The company's owners, Max Blanck and

Isaac Harris, survived because they fled to the roof. They were put on trial but were acquitted because the prosecution failed to prove that the men knew the exit doors were locked at the time of the fire. Blanck and Harris had to compensate $75 per deceased victim, but the insurance company paid the owners about $400 per fatality. To this day, no one knows whether the fire was accidental or was started to claim the insurance money.

The Triangle Shirtwaist Factory fire was a turning point in American history. Countless state and federal laws were enacted because of the horrid incident.

From the wonder and worry of Halley's Comet, talk of birth control, and temperance, to the terrors of the Triangle Shirtwaist Factory fire, the headlines of the time reeled in the background of Mary Matthews's first years at Purdue University and the Gaddis sisters' life together on North Salisbury Street. Slowly, the world was changing for women, but sometimes only after disaster struck. Mary and Lella would soon begin to make their mark to change women's lives in Indiana and beyond.

⸙

In its "parallel universe" on the south side of State Street, the Agricultural Extension Department was growing and changing with each governmental decision. The Clore Act of 1911 created the Department of Agricultural Extension at Purdue and provided $30,000 per year to fund all Extension activities. This allowed the Agricultural Extension Department to become a defined program within the Agricultural Experiment Station. It also brought the end of the Farmers' Institutes as separate entities, for they were no longer an independent branch of the University. Institute work was now a division of the Agricultural Extension Department.

Meanwhile, at the Gaddis home, Kate wrote of the tenants she and Lella hosted. The "Corn School boys" and the "Short Course boys" came and went in the "south room" and the "north room." There were also short courses for young women. At the time under Mary Matthews's tutelage, the Department of Household Economics offered short courses for girls from throughout Indiana. These courses offered practical facts about the art of homemaking and brought Purdue into a closer relationship with women all over the state.

This was when Lella first became friends with George Christie and his family, and she worked various jobs to make ends meet. She cared for the children of her friends, and she was a substitute teacher at Washington School, where Kate taught. Sometimes she substituted for Kate when she had a headache, stomach problems, or aching feet.

> January 27, 1911: Lella out to the Christie's for supper and went with Mrs. C. to the Purdue band concert.

> February 24, 1911: Lella went out and kept Margaret Christie while her mother went to a party.

> April 21, 1911: Lella teaches for Mrs. Staley who has the measles. We both come home footsore and weary.

In the fall of 1912, Mary Matthews, age thirty, was made head of the Department of Household Economics. It was under her tenure that home economics at Purdue emerged as a science. The Department had a total enrollment of fifty young women housed at Ladies Hall. She began with four home economics courses. By this time, the scientific world had made more breakthroughs in nutrition. Casimir Funk, a Polish biochemist, discovered that eating brown rice seemed to prevent beriberi, a disease that can affect the central nervous or cardiovascular systems and cause difficulty in walking, paralysis in the legs, increased heart rate, or more. The substance he found in brown rice that would prevent the disease was Thiamine, which he referred to as a "vitamine." Later this would be known as vitamin B1, and Funk correctly theorized that other diseases could be prevented with vitamins as well. Across the country, home economics schools were blossoming as the need for the understanding of the relationship between nutrition, health, and infant mortality came to be known. It was vital that the knowledge be proclaimed to the masses through education. Mary Matthews's home economics courses became even more important to women and society.

Between the Lines

Kate's diaries flow like sound bites of the era. Startling current events are juxtaposed with warm dinner-table-like conversation about daily chores and the weather. "It's as hot as pepper" and "It's as cold as blue blazes" are two of Kate's favorite weather idioms. At the end of each diary, she keeps a tally of what she spent on clothes she has purchased, sewn, or paid someone else to sew. Clothing was not ready-made in those days, and often Lella and Kate had a seamstress come to the house to fit them for new dresses, or they purchased fabric and made their own garments, right down to gloves, stockings, and panties. She wrote this list in the back of her 1911 black leather diary:

Overshoes	.60
Stockings	.25
Shoes	1.75
Silk dress	3.75
Gingham dress	.94
Pattern	.15

Marta (seamstress)	3.40
Underwear	.20
Gloves	1.20
Hat	6.00
Coat	10.00

Hats were very important then, and Kate mentioned taking her hat in to have it "trimmed." Kate sewed many articles of clothing and home items, which she gave as gifts. In 1912, she listed eighteen "articles made," which included pillowcases, towels, nightgown, aprons, rugs, and doll clothes. Also in the back of her diaries, she sometimes kept a running tab of how much money she gave each week to her church. At the end of 1910, she kept a list of her month-long appointments with the osteopath.

Over the years, Lella and Kate had help with laundry, ironing, and cleaning of their home. It is likely the domestic help they hired were black women. She writes:

> March 27, 1911: Our washerwoman is quite ill. So Lella holds forth in the washer line.

> September 13, 1912: Mrs. McGuinley comes and washes and cleans the house and irons most of the house. Beats Mrs. Smith all to pieces.

The year 1912 proved to be one of great change for the Gaddis sisters. Lella and Kate were struggling a bit financially, and their father was in poor health. They helped serve various dinners to students and staff at Purdue, assumedly for pay. Many of the dinners were for the dignitaries of the University.

> March 6: Pa falls off the porch and about cracks his nose off.

March 13: So mad we have to pay $7.50 back taxes for our Papa.

April 1: We have a *telephone*.

April 16: The Titanaka [sic] the largest vessel ever built was ship wrecked Sunday night, over 1300 lives lost.

Kate misspelled the word "Titanic." How did she hear about the sinking of the ship—by newspaper or word of mouth? It appears that it took two days for the news of the boat hitting the iceberg to reach her. Although telegraphs and newspapers transmitted the story across the globe, it would take time for the word to spread to West Lafayette, Indiana. On May 16, she writes, "Lella hears she has not been getting what she should have for her work here at school."

In the entry above, Kate refers to "here at school." Sometimes she wrote in her diary while she taught her "Little Dears." The teacher for whom Lella substituted had not been honest about payment. Kate, who obviously worried over their finances, expresses her concerns in numerous diary entries:

June 1: Ironed all the clothes. Lella finds out that Miss Matlock has fooled her out of quite a sum of money as she (Miss M.) has been getting $70 per month.

June 17: Went over and registered at Purdue. Will start tomorrow morning.

June 22: Have pictures taken over on Ag steps.

July 5: We are going to serve a dinner to the faculty tomorrow so I offer our dishes, and they are glad to get them.

July 6: Dr. Stone, Miss Winter, Mr. and Mrs. Christie, Mr. and Mrs. Roberts, Miss Shoemaker and Miss Matthews are the guests at the dinner. It goes off fine. Papa is better. Sits up some.

President Winthrop Stone was at the dinner where the Gaddis sisters served, dining on Kate's china, along with Lella's good friends, the

Christies. Mary Matthews, who would become head of the Department of Household Economics that year, also attended the event, along with Carolyn Ernestine Shoemaker, a remarkable Purdue woman. When there was but a smattering of women attending Purdue, Shoemaker earned a Bachelor of Science degree in 1888 and a master's degree the next year. Then twenty-one, she had planned to begin a teaching career, but for the next eleven years, she cared for her incapacitated mother. When her mother died in 1900, Shoemaker returned to Purdue, accepting a position as professor of English literature. She was a calm, poised woman and was a favorite of students.

In 1913, President Stone called Shoemaker to his office and offered her the position of dean of women. Many universities were appointing deans of women, and as he said, he guessed Purdue should, too. Shoemaker was surprised and in awe of such a responsibility, saying she was not sure she could handle such a job. Stone bellowed, "Be a man, Miss Shoemaker! Be a man!" Shoemaker accepted the position. Some years later, Stanley Coulter, dean of men and the dean of the School of Science, said of Shoemaker, "Purdue was not part of her life. Purdue *was* her life." When Purdue called, Shoemaker was there. She was instrumental in the alumni association and a major leader in the building of the Purdue Memorial Union and the struggle for the construction of a women's dormitory. Coulter also said, "her power as a teacher and as a woman lay in the warmth of her feelings." With all due respect to President Stone, Shoemaker knew how to be a *woman.*

For Mary, Lella, and Kate, Shoemaker would have been a wonderful role model akin to Virginia Meredith. Shoemaker, Meredith, and Henrietta Calvin, Mary Matthews's predecessor, were all early examples of how women cared for others, often forced to take time off from their pursuits, while still making great strides in their education, careers, and service to humanity (like women today). Shoemaker aided her mother. Meredith adopted her deceased friend's children. Calvin raised five children while educating herself and eventually became a dean of home economics. And they did it all while wearing ankle-length dresses and enduring the lack of indoor plumbing.

Lella and Kate cared for their increasingly ailing father, aged seventy-two in 1912:

June 24: It is getting hot and going to school is a little hard work. Papa is not feeling well.

June 26: Have a reception for the State Superintendent. We help serve punch and ice cream. When I get home, papa has been very sick and Lella has Dr. Arnett here.

June 27: Papa was very sick all night. We were up with him.

July 2: Have a barber come over today and shave papa for which we pay 60 cents. People are very kind and offer to come and help, but we are better off alone.

⌁

The faculty dinner that Kate referred to on July 6 included the attendance of Margaret Winter. Apparently, she was a love interest of President Stone. Kate writes on July 10, "Dr. Stone and Miss Winter married today. Quite a surprise to all concerned. Does not affect the summer school much, as we do not know them."

President Stone's marriage to Margaret Winter was his second. The year before, he had divorced his first wife, Victoria, on the ground of abandonment. The events leading up to the end of their marriage were startling. It was such shocking news that *The New York Times* ran a story on June 20, 1911:

INDIA CULT CAUSES DIVORCE.

Dr. Stone of Purdue University Deserted by Wife, a Sun Worshipper.

President Stone confirmed a report that his wife had withdrawn from the world, including separation from her husband and family, to pursue a mystic teaching of India known as the philosophy of Yoga. He and his two sons are heartbroken, and would eagerly have welcomed her back but are unable to reach her.

After his wife left him and his two sons to join the "cult" of yoga and become a "sun worshipper," President Stone tendered his resignation to the Purdue University Board of Trustees, but the board voted unanimously to retain Dr. Stone who had been president since 1900. The newspaper goes on to explain how Mrs. Stone became involved in this new "cult":

> Three years ago there was organized in Lafayette a class in so-called Yoga philosophy. . . . It was taught that the complete power of the Yoga involved withdrawal or separation from kindred and friends. . . . it is reported she (Mrs. Stone) has gone to Kabakon, a South Sea island, to join a colony of the new cult. The Kabakon colony is said to be one of the queerest in the world. It was founded several years ago by August Englehardt, and numbers fewer than 100 persons. They live almost entirely on cocoanuts, and the clothing they wear is of the variety and quality affected by the natives in the South Sea Islands who have not come in contact with missionaries. In the South Seas the members of the colony are known as sun worshippers.

One may wonder if Stone's personal turmoil with his wife and her affiliation with a bizarre teaching that led her to abandon her children and home life affected him in such a way that he hesitated to institute home economics courses at Purdue. Did he subconsciously (or consciously) want to keep young women home and married and not teach them more of the world? Victoria was an educated woman who had been a chemist at the Massachusetts State Agricultural Experiment Station before she and Stone married.

❧

As 1912 progressed the health of William Gaddis deteriorated, and Kate and Lella were called upon to care for him around the clock. They were up with him at night and then attempted to sleep and carry on with their lives during the day. Fortunately, Kate was on summer break from her teaching position.

> August 4: Papa is no better. He has such terrible nights. Lella took Pa out for a little ride. He sleeps most of the daytime from the medicine.

August 5: All days seem about the same. Get up and sleep when you can.

August 8: We took Papa to the hospital today. He is getting weak all the time and suffers so.

August 9: Went up to see Papa. He is lots worse. So glad we took him when we did. We went to Mrs. Jones for a party but we did not have a good time for thinking of Papa.

August 11: We both went up to see Papa. He knew us that was all. . . . (We) went back in the afternoon, but he did not know us.

August 12: The Dr. says Papa can't last but a few hours. . . . Mamie and Paul [their sister and nephew] came tonight, but we could not rouse Papa.

August 13: Papa died at 12:25 without a struggle. Such a terrible storm came up before one. We did not get home until almost four. They brought Papa home before suppertime. . . . Lots of people called.

August 14: Mr. and Mrs. Morgan took us out to the cemetery and to get a casket. . . . So many, many people called. Women's Relief Corps had such a nice service this evening at seven.

According to family genealogy records, William Gaddis died of cystitis, an inflammation of the bladder that can be due to bacterial infection. Today cystitis is treated with antibiotics. Of course, such drugs were not available in 1912.

The Women's Relief Corps that Kate refers to was an organization of mothers, sisters, wives, and daughters of Civil War veterans. Kate and Lella apparently were members. The WRC was an auxiliary of the Grand Army of the Republic (GAR), a fraternal organization composed of veterans of the Union Army, as was William Gaddis, who had served in the Civil War. Kate writes on August 15, "We put Papa away today at 10:30 as nice as we could. He did look so nice and there were so many beautiful flowers."

Five days after William passed away, Kate turned forty-four. She commemorates the date, August 19, with the note, "It is my birthday, but we do not celebrate. Institute starts today."

It was also fair time, but Lella and Kate, who usually exhibited their handiwork, did not attend. The sisters began thinking about renting out the room their father had occupied, selecting new wallpaper and preparing the space for another boarder.

> August 26: Have been packing Papa's clothes. Going to take most of them up to the hospital. Sold the bedroom set for $3.00.

> August 27: She [Lella] sent Papa's watch to Clyde [their brother].

❦

The death of William Gaddis was a turning point for Lella and Kate, not just because they lost their "Papa," which was an adjustment in their family life and in their living arrangement since their father occupied their upstairs bedroom, but also because the sisters became more financially secure. They received insurance money after their father passed away. One of the biggest milestones of that year was Lella's admittance into Purdue University as a student. Paul Riley, their nephew, also began classes at Purdue, and he roomed at his aunts' home. At the age of thirty-five, Lella entered college with Paul, age eighteen. Paul majored in poultry and animal husbandry.

> September 10: Lella is going to go to Purdue. She is called in by the Pres. and told she could come this year.

> September 30: We get the insurance $2237.92.

> October 9: We had Miss Matthews over for dinner this evening. Seemed to have a very nice time.

This last entry is interesting because Lella recently started taking classes in Ladies Hall where Mary Matthews had just been made the head of the Department of Household Economics. Was it common to invite your instructor and head of a department to your home for dinner? Would women today invite their college professors home for baked chicken? Of course, the school was much smaller in 1912, and more than likely, people were closer in their relationships. Social lives revolved around visits and "calling" upon friends and coworkers.

Lella and Kate had known Mary since 1910 when she came to campus to work in extension and organize summer school and short courses that they attended. But how well did the three women really know one another? It appears to be a purely teacher/student relationship. Compared to many friends and coworkers mentioned in Kate's diaries, Mary Matthews is referenced rarely. A dinner, tea, or lunch where Mary is present is recorded, and the event sounds obligatory and part of the socially polite way to move in the University circles. Kate writes:

> October 31: Get word the pension has been allowed [presumably from their father]. $100.00. So glad now we can pay most of the debts.

> December 23: We rented the upstairs to a Dr. and his wife and little boy.

Kate ends her 1912 diary with a note about the purchase of land to build a new house: "December 30: Allen telephones he has a chance to loan $1700 at 7% for us on some good land." Their father's insurance money helped them realize a dream.

The Gaddis sisters, Lella, age thirty-five, and Kate, age forty-four, had much to look forward to as their lives changed through Lella's new ventures at Purdue University. With Lella's eventual work, along with Kate's teacher's salary, and the women's combined frugality and savvy business sense as landlords, their financial struggles ended and they built lives of opportunity and joy, always taking time along the way to make meaningful connections with family, friends, neighbors, and Purdue. The women were not paid much, and of course, not nearly what a man would have been paid at that time, but the rent they collected along with their thrift enabled them to live comfortable lives. The Gaddis's were educated women, living without husbands, purchasing property, and taking care of themselves in a time when women had few rights, were expected to raise a family, stay at home, and depend upon a man. Often, the single woman of the 1910s was looked upon as an object of pity. But not Lella and Kate.

Water under the Bridge

There are newspaper stories, books, and photographs that give detailed and telling descriptions of Lafayette's structurally devastating flood in 1913, but Kate's diary gives a personal glimpse of what it was like to live through the greatest natural disaster in the history of Lafayette and West Lafayette, Indiana. She writes on March 21, "Friday rolls around and a big storm at 6 this morning. A man killed in front of Foster's Furniture Store. Fences down and lots of roofs off buildings."

Easter Sunday was two days later, and Kate wrote that it poured all day. The rain kept coming, and the Wabash River continued to rise. She continues:

> March 24: Still raining. Go to school and take no umbrella so have to borrow Rosie Merrill's old cotton one but am glad to get it.
>
> March 25: When we went over, the river seemed high. Before time to come home, the bridge was roped off.
>
> March 26: Brown Street Bridge partly gone. School dismissed on account of no water. Gas off. Water highest in history. Main Street Bridge is sinking.

For seven days the Wabash River swelled, gulping up structures that stood in its path. The river level rose to thirty-three feet. The gushing water swept away all buildings on the Main Street Levee (where Wabash Landing is today). West Lafayette was dependent upon Lafayette for electricity, gas, telephones, food, and water, so the town was virtually isolated when the bridges were gone. Normally, Kate traveled by streetcar from West Lafayette to Washington School in Lafayette. But when the river rose, streetcar service was suspended because its tracks ran alongside the doomed Main Street Bridge. Debris from demolished buildings and the swelling water pounded against the piers of the bridge, causing authorities to fear its demise. Eventually, the bridge buckled under the pressure of the water and the western span sank. The Brown Street Bridge had been the first to crumble under the force of the current.

In an attempt to hold the Big Four Railroad Bridge in place, loaded coal cars were pulled onto the span. The added weight kept the railroad bridge from being swept away, but it was knocked five inches out of line by floating buildings. When the railroad bridge was the only connecting link between the two towns, some Purdue students jumped from coal car to coal car to cross the flooded river and visit their girlfriends in Lafayette.

For months after the flood, citizens crossed the Wabash on a cable-drawn ferry. Because there was no gas line or telephone service at their home, Lella and Kate stayed overnight at homes of relatives and friends in Lafayette until life return to normal. Kate writes:

> March 30: We had quite a few oxen in the ditch today. Do not go to church this morning. The gas comes on again today. Water going down some.
>
> April 2: RR Bridge condemned and the only way across the river is by boat.
>
> April 5: Get over home on the ferry a little after nine this morning. Have lots of things to do and am busy. Ferry goes wrong this p.m. They found the boy who drowned a week ago.

Lella and Kate Gaddis crossed the Wabash River on a cable-drawn ferry when the bridges collapsed during the Flood of 1913 in Lafayette, Indiana. Kate wrote in her diary, "We get so tired climbing up and down the bank of the old river." Courtesy of Tippecanoe County Historical Association.

April 7: Go to school by way of small boats as the ferry is not running. Come home the same way. The river is about the busiest place.

April 8: Climbing the bank to the river is a little muddy and slippery

April 18: We walk across the Main Street Bridge this morning but it is closed by evening.

May 12: Nothing much happens, although we get so tired climbing up and down the bank of the old river. Tired out before we get to school.

May 16: We go to J. Wades to the Young Women's Guild. Come home for the first time at night on the ferry. Beautiful moonlight.

October 1: Cars go across the bridge for the first time since March.

By Kate's account, it took six months for the Main Street Bridge to reopen to traffic after the historic flood. Today, as cars zoom across one of the concrete bridges that span the Wabash River on the way to or from West Lafayette, it is hard to imagine traversing the water in a wooden boat or by cable-drawn ferry. Kate and Lella climbed down the muddy bank in ankle-length skirts while keeping their feathered plumed hats atop their heads. They stepped onto a crowded boat that sliced the river current and reached the other side after about a ten-minute voyage. At night with the moon shining above, a boat ride on the Wabash would have been a lovely sight, yet a sharp contrast to the surrounding destruction.

Ironically, the Indiana General Assembly adopted "On the Banks of the Wabash, Far Away" by songwriter Paul Dresser as the official state song on March 14, 1913, just days before the swollen Wabash River changed the course of everyday life for Lafayette citizens for half of that year. Dresser wrote the ballad as a reminiscence of his mother and his childhood home along the Wabash River in Terre Haute, Indiana, south of Lafayette. The chorus is what Hoosiers may know most:

> Oh, the moonlight's fair tonight along the Wabash,
> From the fields there comes the breath of new mown hay.
> Through the sycamores the candlelights are gleaming,
> On the banks of the Wabash, far away.

After the passing of the Clore Act of 1911, extension services expanded and land-grant colleges were looking for qualified people to become extension workers. A couple of universities came calling on Lella Gaddis. Here is Kate's record of Lella's experience with West Virginia University in Morgantown, West Virginia:

> May 8, 1913: While she [Lella] is away, has a telephone message from a man in West Virginia who wants her to consider an appointment in the collage [sic] there. He called in the evening.

May 29: Lella's birthday. She has a letter from West. Va. offering to pay half her expenses down.

June 7: Lella gets a telegram to be in Morganston [sic] at 11:30 Monday morning. We have to get a suit and take out insurance. Miss Matthews here for supper.

June 8: Lella leaves at 4 p.m.

June 11: Commencement at Purdue. Lella gets home none the wiser for her trip, but had a good time.

June 23: We are all up and at the cherries this morning. Have a bushel and a half done by eight o'clock. Lella has not heard from West Va. yet.

June 30: Lella has a letter from West Va. for her to sign her expenses.

Lella traveled to West Virginia University for a job interview. She bought a new suit and took out insurance before she headed south. Did the two women worry that something would befall Lella on her solo trip? The diaries do not indicate how Lella traveled to West Virginia. It is likely she took the train. While Lella is willing to pursue the exciting adventure of leaving West Lafayette and embark into unknown territories at a different university in another state, Kate has an invitation of her own that year, but fails to follow through. She commented on May 26 that after her additional schooling at Purdue, she obtained a twenty-four-month teaching license in sewing and a twelve-month license in cooking. She "can teach anyplace in the state." Kate writes on September 25, "Get a letter from Indianapolis Schools with an application blank. Don't know if I want to fill it out and send it back or not. Nellie Barrett from West Va. visits Purdue today."

There is no indication as to who Nellie Barrett was. Perhaps she was the person Lella saw on her trip. Kate did not say what was written in Lella's last letter from West Virginia University received on July 9, and no more mention is made of Lella's interview there. If only we knew what Lella thought of her experience at West Virginia's land-grant college. In her eyes, how did it compare to Purdue University?

One may wonder if Mary Matthews knew of Lella's interview with West Virginia. Kate indicated that Mary ate supper with the sisters the day the telegram was delivered telling when Lella was to be in Morgantown. There are several mentions of Mary in the 1913 diary, perhaps because Lella was then a full-time student in the Department of Household Economics, while Kate was a summer school student, and the three women had become more familiar.

Kate mentioned that Lella helped Mary with a lunch for the senior girls, and they used the sisters' dishes "for the spread." In June, Mary had the Home Economics students "on the lawn for a social." Lella and Mary had dinner together four times in 1913. Kate took up basket making as a pastime. She must have given Mary one of her creations, for she wrote, "Get such a nice letter from Miss Matthews thanking me for the basket." Kate's entry on the day after Columbus Day was quirky. She said, "I sent Miss Matthews a card telling her it was a shame she did not land with Columbus." It appeared that the Gaddis sisters and Mary were becoming closer.

❦

Ever topical in her literary pursuits, Kate was reading a book that was published that year, *Laddie: A True Blue Story* by Gene Stratton-Porter, who was from Wabash, Indiana. After she married a druggist from Geneva, Indiana, and the family literally "struck oil," Stratton-Porter used their wealth to design and build a fourteen-room home near the Limberlost Swamp. It was there, amid nature's bounty, that Stratton-Porter photographed birds and animals in their habitat and sent her pictures to *Recreation* magazine. This began her career as a writer, for the magazine asked her to pen a column about cameras. Encouraged by her magazine endeavors, she turned to writing fiction and wrote several novels that included descriptions of natural settings, including *A Girl of the Limberlost*. In 1913 after the Limberlost Swamp had been drained, Stratton-Porter moved to Rome City where she built "The Cabin at Wildflower Woods." Today it is the location of the Gene Stratton-Porter Historic Site.

Laddie was said to be the most autobiographical of Stratton-Porter's books. She was the youngest of twelve children, and her mother died when she was five. Two quotes from the novel speak of the author's commentary on women and her conviction of family. One could believe that Lella or Kate wrote these lines:

> This world must have her women quite as much as her men. It is shoulder to shoulder, heart to heart, business. (p. 257)

> Families were made to cling together, and stand by each other in every circumstance of life—joy or sorrow. (p. 370)

❧

Every fall when Purdue began the first semester of the school year, Kate wrote, "Tank scrap is on." Tank scrap was an annual tradition that began when the class of 1889 painted a large "89" on the steeple of the old Agricultural Building. The faculty objected to the defacing of their building, so the tradition moved off campus to a fifty-foot water tower at the top of Salisbury Street hill. Freshman would paint their numerals on the tank, as high as they could, and the sophomores would try to remove the younger boys. A battle would ensue from midnight to daybreak, and the class that tied up all the members of the other class won. They would then strip the losers to their underwear, dump wagon paint on them, and parade them around a bonfire and through town. This was all considered good fun, and the tank scrap continued as an annual fall tradition until 1913 when Francis W. Obenchain from South Whitley, Indiana, died due to a broken neck. Lella and Kate's nephew Paul was there. Kate writes on September 19, "Tank scrap on. Paul gets the wind knocked out of him. Openshane [sic] died."

Kate misspelled Obenchain's name. Probably, she had just heard his name and not seen it in writing. *The New York Times* ran a story with the headline "College sued for $25,000. Purdue University Officials Blamed for Death Caused by Hazing." Obenchain's father sued Purdue alleging, "That the tank scrap was brutal, degrading and a vicious fight, having the purpose of inflicting injuries upon new students." The day after Obenchain's death, the classes voted to abolish the tank scrap.

Many times in her diaries, Kate mentioned various illnesses that affected the schoolchildren and teachers at Washington School. Most of these sicknesses were ones that we no longer fear in the United States due to vaccines, knowledge, and better nutrition. In 1913, the school was closed because of a diphtheria scare. A vaccine for diphtheria was not widely available until the 1930s. Throughout history, diphtheria was a leading cause of death among children and was once referred to as the "strangling angel of children." Kate writes:

> November 11: School ordered closed on account of diphtheria for rest of the week at best.
>
> November 16: No church on account of diphtheria scare.
>
> November 19: School begins again today. Scare over.

For many months of 1913, Kate jotted down notes about their Uncle Alder's battle with malaria, which is transmitted by mosquitoes. Did the flood of 1913 increase the number of mosquitoes and therefore affect the incidence of malaria? On December 19 she stated, "Uncle Alder not doing so well. His liver is out of fix."

Even Lella and Kate's dog was affected by the lack of vaccines that are commonplace today.

> July 31: Rex and a bulldog have a fight. Boy has his hand bitten.
>
> August 6: Rexie goes to the Happy Hunting Ground last evening. Dog had rabies that bit him.

Kate made no more mention of the boy who was bitten.

At the end of the 1913 diary, there is a list entitled "People eating at our house this year." The tally of names of friends, family, and coworkers and the dates they dined at the Gaddis home gives a sense of the openness and hospitable ways of Lella and Kate. Month by month, the list progressed with a total at each month's end: "January, 37 meals"; "March, 50 meals"; "November, 56 meals." At the end of the December list, Kate wrote, "400 meals besides ourselves in 1913." Lella and Kate would host many a luncheon, dinner, tea, and child's birthday party in the years to come. They were frugal, yet generous with meals for the ones they loved, honored, and respected.

No Blue Monday

The Gaddis sisters' Uncle Alder succumbed to malaria in 1914. His death on January 1 took Kate to the cemetery with her Aunt Vera. Throughout the year, Kate visited and had dinner with her "lonesome" and "unhappy" aunt. The year continued to be one of sickness for the family, yet also a milestone in the making. Later in the month, Kate wrote of her latest book: "Am reading 'Hoosier Chronicle.' Very good."

Hoosier Chronicle by Meredith Nicholson was published in 1912. Nicholson was born in Crawfordsville, Indiana, and he wrote about varied topics from politics to the environment. In *Hoosier Chronicle*, Nicholson conveyed his deep pride for his native state.

January also brought a smallpox scare. It was very cold at that time, and Kate talked of Lella purchasing a new coat. On January 17, she writes, "We go over and get Lella a coat much to her disgust, as she does not like the cut this year."

Lella was an impeccable dresser her entire life. In her later years, when apparel became ready-made, she did not buy many articles of clothing, but when she did, she bought quality. She wore her clothes well with her stately posture.

On February 3, Kate made her first mention of Virginia Meredith. She writes, "Lella helps 'Auntie Meredith' make a basket." Mary Matthews called her mother "Auntie," and Lella and Kate referred to Virginia by that term of endearment. It was common for young people to call an older woman "Auntie," even if the woman was not truly their aunt. This is why many mistakenly thought Virginia Meredith was Mary Matthews's real aunt, when in fact she was her adoptive mother only and not a blood relative.

Kate wrote frequently of Lella attending Purdue football and basketball games, often with their nephew Paul. She always included the scores, yet never mentioned that she attended, until 1914, and it sounds as if she was not fond of bleachers: "March 6, 1914: Went to see my first basketball game. Purdue beats 28 to 15 with Minn. Sat around and almost broke my back."

Anna Roberta McNeill lived near the Gaddis home. Lella and Kate were quite fond of her. McNeill (or "Mack" as Kate called her) worked at Purdue helping with the Farmers' Institutes and working as a home demonstration agent. She was from Canada and had been a student of the Macdonald Institute, which was part of the Ontario Agricultural College. The Institute was established in 1903 to provide higher education to rural women in home management skills. The Institute became part of the University of Guelph, and later its name was changed to the College of Family and Consumer Studies. George Christie, director of Purdue's Department of Agricultural Extension, was also a graduate of Ontario Agricultural College. Perhaps he hired McNeill having known her through their alma mater.

Mack often ate supper with the sisters at their kitchen table, staying afterward to play cards. In March, her doctor told McNeill that she had to go to the hospital. Kate did not write why Mack was hospitalized, but their friend was distraught. Kate writes, "March 29: Miss McNeill down for supper. She is boo-hooing about going. We do not let her talk of it."

Kate visited Mack several times while she was in the hospital for a couple of weeks.

> April 9: Miss Matthews asked me to go to the hospital.

> April 10: I went to see Miss M. Not very satisfactory as Miss Matthews was there.

It is curious as to why Kate's visit with her friend Mack was "not very satisfactory" in the presence of Mary Matthews. Did Kate feel awkward visiting her sick friend as Mary looked on? Did Mary's bedside manner fall short? Perhaps there was tension concerning McNeill's work in home economics extension through the School of Agriculture—a tension that would soon affect Lella.

Beginning the first week of May 1914, Kate's handwriting changed from the tiny, neat penmanship she usually displayed, to script that was scrawled and a bit helter-skelter. Kate was sick.

> May 7: Am not feeling at all well.

> May 8: Have such a lot of pains. I can hardly stand it till we get home to go to bed.

For the next month, Kate stayed home and did not go to school to teach her "Little Dears." Friends, family, and coworkers called throughout the time and brought tulips, pink rosebuds, daisies, and lily of the valley. It is obvious by the number of people who visited that there was concern about Kate's health. Many also telephoned.

> May 11: My, I feel too mean for words. Lella goes to school and I sleep most of the day.

> May 12: Rains all day, but I hardly hear it as I am contented sleeping. Time goes awful fast when in the arms of Morpheas.

In Greek Mythology, Morpheas or Morpheus is the god of dreams. Morpheus sends images of humans in dreams or visions and is responsible for shaping dreams. The drug morphine is named after Morpheus for its ability to make one sleepy and dreamy. Kate's reference to Morpheus speaks of her well-read persona.

McNeill returned the favor of the hospital "sick-bed" vigil by staying with Kate many times during her illness, particularly when Lella was absent. The doctor paid a few house calls as well.

> May 20: Lady Mc. (McNeill) down. I tell her she can come stay with us if she wants to.
>
> May 25: Do not feel able to go to school yet. Am only up part of the time. This getting well seems to go mighty slow.

Throughout Kate's illness, Lella continued to attend guild meetings, dinners at Purdue, basketball games, and other social and work events. Perhaps she asked their friend McNeill to stay with Kate so she could attend functions knowing her big sister was in good company. No grass grew under Lella's feet, so staying home with her sister may have been something she could only experience in small doses. The sisters-of-opposites worked out a living arrangement that answered both of their needs.

> May 28: I go to school but things are in a muss. Children glad to see me back. Teachers are so pleased.
>
> May 29: Go to school again today. Principal tells me how mean she feels because she has worked me to death. Glad she knows it.

This last line reveals Kate's personality. The fact of the matter is, Kate was sickly, and it influenced her demeanor. Lella was younger and more robust than her sister. Throughout her diaries, the tone of Kate's commentary sometimes took on a "why me?" attitude. Yet she could be funny and loving, especially with regard to children. She never slighted Lella for her endeavors at Purdue, in clubs, with friends, or with other outside activities. The sisters lived with mutual respect.

Kate had another setback after her May 29 entry and stayed home for the remainder of the school year. Lella acted as a substitute teacher for her, and Kate commented that she was so sorry her sister could not rest during the last week of school. It appeared that Kate was required to pay the women who substituted for her, so perhaps having Lella sub saved Kate money. McNeill moved her trunks into the Gaddis home. Kate was happy to have her live with them.

June 11: Tomorrow ends the school. I feel now like I never want to see another.

June 12: I went over and handed out the tickets (for promotions). Little Dears glad to see me. The board pays Miss Ellenga one week. So I only have to hand out $25 to her.

In later years, Kate would be diagnosed with diabetes and thyroid disease. Little was known about how to treat diabetes in 1914. It was just in 1910 that the chemical produced by the pancreas had been dubbed "insulin." In 1922, the first diabetic patient was treated with an injection of insulin.

As sick as Kate was during the spring of 1914, she continued to write in her diary every day. Perhaps her journal was a sort of therapy for her, a way to put down her inner thoughts and cope with each day. She was an educated teacher, a well-read woman, and she expressed herself through the written word. How much of what she wrote did she convey verbally? Did she believe that someday someone would read her tomes and thread together her life and the life of her sister?

In June, Lella helped in Mary Matthews's Purdue summer school, and she received two out-of-state job prospects.

June 15: Summer school starts today, and Lella is assisting busy as a bee. She had a letter from Penn. asking her to let them know if she would consider a $1200 job.

June 21: We are at Miss Matthews for a picnic lunch. Have a very nice time. I am so awful tired when we get home.

Kate was included in many of the Department of Household Economics lunches and socials that Lella attended. Did Mary Matthews know of Lella's extension department job offer at Penn State? Perhaps so, because the next month Kate wrote, "Miss Matthews tells Lella to keep it quiet, but she is going to have a job doing extension work. My but I am glad now she will be at home or 'in and out.'" Kate later adds on

Mary L. Matthews was in her third year as head of the Department of Household Economics when this photo was taken in 1915. These are the highly educated women of the department (left to right): Alice Biester, Loretta Mae Wallace, Amy Lord Howe, Mary Lockwood Matthews, Mary Edith Gamble, and Miriam Sarah Roberts. Not shown, but included in the yearbook with the names of the above women were Anna Roberta McNeill, close friend and boarder of the Gaddis sisters, and Lella Reed Gaddis. Both were listed as having positions in home economics extension. Courtesy of Purdue University Libraries, Archives and Special Collections.

July 22, "Miss McNeill seems most as pleased as if it were she who has a job, when Miss Matthews tells her. We had not said anything to her."

McNeill was probably happy about Lella's new job as state leader of home demonstration because she would be the assistant home demonstration agent working with her good friend.

Months passed, Kate became stronger, and Lella continued working for Mary. She was responsible for setting up an exhibit at the Indiana State Fair in September and stayed there for the week. Kate writes on September 7, "Lella gets her notice from the President of the collage [sic]. She is to have $900. Not to be sneezed at, I tell you. It may be Blue Monday for some, but not for us."

Penn State offered Lella $1,200 dollars a year, while Purdue offered her $900 to take a position as the state leader of home demonstration. Lella chose to accept Purdue's lower monetary offer. In 2010, Lella's great-niece, Miriam Epple-Heath, explained, "Lella decided to stay at Purdue even though she would earn less, because she realized how her life and other's lives would change if she moved."

It is likely when making her choice, Lella thought most of her sister. Kate had a good teaching position of her own. There was Kate's health to consider and the obvious fact that Kate did not like change. If Lella accepted the position with Penn State, she would have to leave a long list of friends and family. Lella chose relationships over money.

Kate felt well enough to start school in the fall. It was a good thing that her health had improved, for she had forty "Little Dears" in her classroom, as she explained, "We have the largest enrollment we have ever had. Miss Ullrick has 50, making 90 in the first grade."

Lella began traveling right away in a Model T, carrying her demonstration suitcase that held what she needed to teach better ways of performing home tasks. In the first few weeks of her job, she was off to Indianapolis, Logansport, Noblesville, and Crawfordsville. McNeill also traveled as part of her extension work. They set up in courthouses, schools, and on farms to teach eager rural women new methods in homemaking skills. Mothers of large families were responsible for a vast array of essential household and farm chores. They worked long hours using techniques handed down from their mothers. Little if any information was written down as reference. These countrywomen were overworked and tired, yet they had a strong desire to better their family's lives. Their minds were fertile ground for learning the scientific and academic lessons the extension agents brought from Purdue. These mothers and wives were hungry for the formation of "Home Economics Clubs," and the social and friendship aspects of these clubs were added joys.

Kate wrote of the individual comings and goings of Lella and Mack. She kept track of when the women left home, their destinations, how long they were gone, and the time, to the minute, that they returned.

October 14: This is the week of the County Agents Institute. Both the ladies busy attending.

October 20: Lella is out with Mr. Hooker visiting "country schools."

In later years, Lella described what her state leader of home demonstration position was like in the beginning:

> I couldn't possibly have been trained for the work, because it was yet to be developed. Dr. Christie, Director of Extension, had confidence in my ability to discover the needs of the people and devise a way to meet the needs. I was in my early thirties. I had abundant energy with good health and courage to tackle the job. I came from a farm home and knew farm conditions. The women worked hard to feed and clothe their families and helped with the farm work in many instances. In the fall of 1914, I attended all meetings and public events I could to contact women and learn from them their needs in homemaking skills and to let them know that we would hold meetings to instruct. One of the strengths of the program was that it was based on the needs of the people. Never to my knowledge did we ever say, "We will teach this lesson because it will be good for them." (Thompson, *Fifty Years of Extension*, pp. 54-55)

Lella's new position took some of the financial pressure off Kate. She felt ill again in November and states, "I feel so badly I do not go to school. My, it seems nice to think you can stay home if you are sick and not break the Bank of Monte Carlo." She follows on November 17, "Lella goes off with Pa Latta today at 6:30 to Ellettsville. She will be gone all week."

Lella and Kate referred to Professor William Latta, then sixty-four, as "Pa." It seems Lella's bond with the men of the School of Agriculture was ever growing with her new position in home economics extension.

The Gaddis sisters continued to save money to build a new home and think of their financial future even through their Christmas gift giving. These enterprising women also purchased a home to rent on Grant Street. Kate writes:

> December 7: We get a mortgage through the Building and Loan for $1800 on 116 S. Grant St. property at 5 ½ percent.
>
> December 21: Get Lella a share in the Building and Loan.

Women watch a dress form demonstration at the 1921 Lawrence County Farmer's picnic held at Moses Annex Farm near Bedford, Indiana. Home demonstrations were as much a social event as a learning experience. Courtesy of Purdue University Libraries, Archives and Special Collections.

There was no mention in Kate's 1914 diary of the clandestine night when the Ag Boys hitched up their horse and buggy and moved Lella's office out of Ladies Hall. On December 3 when Lella was gone for the week, Kate wrote a rather cryptic note: "Have a letter from Lella. Things don't seem so bad now."

There was no explanation for the mysterious entry. Did Lella tell Kate about her office moving from Mary Matthews's department over to Agricultural Extension? If Lella mentioned it in passing without much fanfare, would it be of much significance to Kate? After all, Lella's headquarters were now in the Agricultural Experiment Station and near the offices of her friends, John Skinner and George Christie.

(Lella and Kate even spent part of Christmas Day at the Skinner home, as they would for many years to come.) Lella felt at ease with these men and the mission of the Department of Agricultural Extension. She traveled all over the state to teach rural women, and she did not spend much time in her office. Lella's job was on the road.

Mary Matthews was the one working on campus, scraping together funds and support to build her department and teach home economics to women students. Technically, she had been the first Purdue home demonstration agent hired by Christie in 1910. She had first-hand knowledge of home economics extension work. In Mary's view, as the first state leader of home demonstration, Lella Gaddis, should have been in her realm. Lella had worked the summer before as an assistant in Mary's summer school classes. Many of the teachings in Mary's department would be what Lella would carry forth to rural women who were unable to attend college. The rub was the money. Mary needed appropriations to expand her Department of House-hold Economics. The appropriations for home economics extension moved when Lella moved. The "Ag Boys" would get the money Mary sorely needed.

Mary Matthews may have felt betrayal. Lella had taken classes and worked in the Department of Household Economics. She was very connected with the group in Ladies Hall. At that time, there were few women faculty members and students at Purdue, and the small circle of females all knew one another. Mary had spoken in confidence with Lella, allowing her to be privy to guarded information regarding the news that she might get the extension job. Understandably, when she gave Lella advanced notice, Mary thought the state leader of home demonstration position was part of her department. Mary had no way of knowing she would be blindsided later. After the men in the Department of Agricultural Extension moved Lella's desk and files across State Street, Lella crossed over to the other side, literally and figuratively, and perhaps in Mary's eyes became one of the "Ag Boys." As a woman and head of a department for women, Mary had little power and no choice. To borrow from Kate's phraseology, for Mary Matthews it *was* a "Blue Monday."

Practice the Art

After Mary Matthews was named head of the Department of Household Economics, she worked to develop her own way to bring more women to Purdue and cultivate her program. At the time, most of the men at Purdue did not want women "cluttering up the campus." Mary's brother, Meredith, was a Sigma Chi when he attended Purdue. Mary learned from Meredith that members of his fraternity did not approve of taking coeds to any functions. This "anti-women" attitude was also reflected in the faculty. Mary and her mother, Virginia, recognized that they needed to interest people of the state in supporting the home economics program. That impetus promoted their creation of the Indiana Home Economics Association (IHEA).

Still today, even with the changes in women's roles, thousands of women are members of Home Economics Clubs. Here is where Mary Matthews and Lella Gaddis worked toward the same goal, on different sides of the fence. Every Home Economics Club in Indiana was born of the groundwork set by Mary Matthews and Virginia Meredith as they formed a blanket organization for all Indiana Home Economics Clubs, but also by Lella Gaddis as she traveled the state training ordinary farm women to be leaders to form Home Economics or Demonstration Clubs within their counties. On January 17, 1913, during the Agricultural Conference at Purdue, Mary and Virginia called a small group of women together to discuss the possibility of organizing an IHEA to encourage more county educational groups for homemakers and to promote the teaching of domestic science in local schools. The group of women met in William Latta's office. A temporary constitution was drawn, and Virginia read a skeleton document, which was adopted at the meeting. Virginia Meredith was elected president and Mary Matthews was a member of the executive committee. In addition, the members felt that they needed the input of a man, so George Christie also was elected a member of the executive committee. Amy Lord Howe was made temporary secretary. Howe was an instructor working for Mary in the Department of Household Economics.

According to the Indiana Home Demonstration Association's fiftieth anniversary commemorative booklet, which was published in 1963 and spearheaded by Mrs. W. G. DePew, who served as chairman, fifty-eight women became members that day. Many of the women who first joined the IHEA were Farmers' Institute speakers. These members fostered and expanded the work of Purdue and the fledgling association. Leaders in the counties worked diligently to begin classes for farm women and girls. These Home Economics Clubs later became known as Home Demonstration Clubs. The girls' groups became 4-H clubs. The IHEA members and county leaders also worked to petition for legislation that would establish funds and offices for the early extension workers in each county. In essence, the IHEA became a lobbying force for women, extension, and home economics, while providing farm women with an educational and social group to which they could connect.

The IHEA furthered Mary Matthews's ties and good works to promote home economics extension, as well as home economics. The IHEA was a groundbreaking, profoundly influential entity for women that would grow monumentally for decades to come, launching thousands of clubs around the state, many of which still exist today. The IHEA was another example of Mary's close ties with extension work. In light of what we know about the events of 1914 and the shift of Lella's office from the Department of Household Economics to the School of Agriculture, one can understand Mary's ill feeling toward the "Ag Boys" who took what she deemed part of her mission.

A year later in the 1914 minutes of the IHEA, it was moved that a "night letter" be sent by the association to their congressman urging passage of the Smith-Lever Act. A night letter was a telegram sent at nighttime at a reduced rate for delivery the next morning. The IHEA was a strong supporter of the establishment of extension. In President Virginia Meredith's message that year, she said, "Every community needs organized groups of women to guide, in a common- sense way, spirited discussions about whatever will make Indiana homes better homes. " Mrs. J. M. Hamilton of Franklin County spoke of the "advancing interest of farmwomen in the efficiency of their homes and the organization of Domestic Science Clubs arising from home economics lectures and demonstrations given in their locality during a short course."

The next year at the third annual meeting of the association, President Winthrop Stone was the speaker. His topic was "The Future of Home Economics at Purdue." He told his listeners that home economics at Purdue was not a "fad" and that Purdue did not cater to young women who go to college for "social diversion." These are interesting comments given his first wife was infatuated with a "fad" as a "sun worshipper" and left her family for what one might deem a "social diversion." Professor Latta was added to the executive committee that year, but by 1917, both Christie and Latta were eliminated, making the group an all-female entity.

At the annual meeting held in 1916, the minutes indicate that Anna Roberta McNeill (Lella and Kate's friend who was by then their boarder and coworker) reported 127 home economics "study classes." This was the first year that the clubs around the state sent delegates to the meeting. In addition, that year, Virginia Meredith moved from her farm in Cambridge City to West Lafayette to live with her daughter at 356 West State Street. Virginia was sixty-seven when she began living close to the Purdue campus. Her move would mark another prominent chapter in her life and solidify her ties and influence with Purdue even more. Her presence also would help her daughter in their shared mission of advancing women in society and at home through the development of home economics as a respected field of study at Purdue. According to Mary Louise Krichbaum, whose family had an egg route and made a delivery each Saturday to Virginia and Mary, the mother and daughter duo created a beautiful home together and always displayed a fresh bouquet of roses in their living room.

A gavel made from yellow poplar was presented to the IHEA in 1941. It was a gift from Mrs. T. Eugene Bailey and was made by her brother from a stairway of their old home in Tippecanoe county. Lella Gaddis, who often did intricate woodcarving, engraved the gavel.

In 1951, the IHEA became known as the Indiana Home Demonstration Association, and today it is the Indiana Extension Homemakers Association (IEHA). In 1963, when the Association celebrated its fiftieth year, there were 3,059 clubs with 65,000 Hoosier homemakers "striving to apply knowledge to homemaking." In the early 1980s, the IEHA had 44,539 members statewide. As times changed and more women worked outside the home, membership declined by almost 50%, and the number of clubs decreased throughout the state. Yet the IEHA's mission to strengthen families through continuing education, leadership development, and volunteer community support remains a vital commodity in today's world. Now women have more choices and avenues to realize these kinds of goals, be it through their careers, a varied offering of volunteer opportunities, or on the Internet.

Most of the photos of Mary Matthews picture a stern, matronly looking woman with her wavy hair pinned tightly to her head. People described her as "reserved," yet she has also been depicted in the *Debris* yearbook and various magazine and newspaper stories as an attractive, merry woman. A story written by Caroline B. King in August 1944 for "The Economist" newsletter states:

> Her life has been rich and vivid, she has spread good cheer and happiness along with learning. She has helped hundred of girls and women, yes and men too, over seemingly insurmountable difficulties, encouraging them to greater efforts and enduring success, and throughout all her endeavors preserved the sunniness [sic], the sparkle, the good humor which are synonymous with the name of Mary Matthews.

Throughout her career, Mary was, in a sense, "competing" with the men of the School of Agriculture. In 2010, Purdue Dean Emeritus of the School of Home Economics Eva Goble explained, "They [men of

Pictured are the first students to live in the home economics Practice House instituted by Mary Matthews in 1919. She was the acting supervisor in the House. At that time, Practice Houses were a new educational tool in home economics departments at colleges and universities around the country. Courtesy of Purdue University Libraries, Archives and Special Collections.

the School of Agriculture] were trying to get home economics as part of the Ag. The men controlled the money. Dean Matthews said, 'If I'm going to train these people, it seems I should have the money in my budget.' Which was reasonable. The men didn't think so."

Because many of the "Ag Boys" wanted the money that was appropriated to the Department of Household Economics, Mary had to stick to her guns to keep on top of the funding. Perhaps this is why at times she came across as stern. She had to be smart and cautious while persevering in her effort to build her department and educate women.

The rapid growth of Purdue's Department of Household Economics was due to Mary's untiring efforts and innovative ideas. When she became head of the department in 1912, there was a total enrollment of forty girls. Home economics was housed in Ladies Hall for the next eleven years, and later in a building that once was next door called the Biology Annex. Mary's leadership began with a staff of three instructors and an assistant. By the time she retired in 1952, Mary was responsible for twenty-five faculty members.

❧

When classes began in the fall of 1919, Mary Matthews debuted a new way of learning for the young women of the Department of Household Economics. It was called the "Practice House." She wrote about the new educational endeavor in *The Purdue Agriculturist*, a monthly publication of Purdue's School of Agriculture. She explained, "The Practice House is a laboratory arranged to afford each senior student in Home Economics an opportunity for practice in the management of a home." The purpose of the Practice House, also known as the Home Management House, was to "establish standards of right living" and provide a hands-on environment for the student to practice what she had been taught in the classroom. A nine-room structure that previously housed the Alpha Chi Omega Sorority at 115 Waldron Street was rented by Purdue University. The students planned and purchased the furnishings.

The "family" in the house was a group of six students and a chaperone. Each student lived in the house for thirty days and during that time acted in six capacities—hostess, housekeeper, assistant housekeeper, cook, assistant cook, and waitress. Each title came with duties that were assigned in five-day increments. For instance, the cook was responsible for all preparation and service of meals, cleaning the refrigerator once in five days, and baking "good yeast bread once during the five days." Each hostess was to arrange to have guests once during her term. The waitress polished silver and laundered doilies, among other dining room responsibilities such as dishwashing. The supervisor checked all work each day.

Each girl paid $10 monthly rent for room, gas, and electricity, and she paid for the cost of the food, which was eighteen to twenty-three cents per meal. The students continued to take classes while they lived and worked in the Practice House. Mary wrote, "[The students] manage their work in the house so that it does not interfere [with their studies], nor does it 'wear them out.' As many labor-saving appliances as possible are used such as a fireless gas stove, a kitchen cabinet, a high stool, a wheel tray and a suction sweeper."

At the time, Practice Houses were springing up as a new educational tool in home economics departments at colleges and universities around the country. On March 14, 1920, the *Indianapolis Star* featured an article entitled "Purdue University's New Practice House" written by Mabel L. Harlan of the Department of Agricultural Extension. At that time, Mary was the acting supervisor at the house. This article summarized what each girl was to bring with her for her stay: one wash housedress, white aprons, colored aprons, towels, and bedding. In her diary of that year, Kate Gaddis mentioned going to the Practice House for dinner.

The 1920s were developmental years for home economics. Mary created departments, found instructors for those departments, and implemented current trends in teaching. The department's rapid growth called for a new building. In 1922, the red brick Home Economics Building, today called Matthews Hall, was constructed at the corner of West State and University Streets. The streetcar ran down the center of both streets, flanking the Classical Revival style structure. The building featured laboratories for teaching foods, clothing, dietetics, food chemistry, and textile chemistry. The new building also featured an auditorium with seating for three hundred. Today the auditorium is the oldest on campus. The building's cafeteria, called the "Spruce Room," so named for the spruce trees that grew outside its doors, provided a training laboratory for students in institutional management. At the time, Purdue was one of few colleges and universities that offered a food service organization in which students worked. It began in 1918 with a challenge from President Stone. He said he would give his permission for a "group feeding" class if it did not cost Purdue "one cent." The class served two lunches per week and never once operated at a loss. Each student was required to sell 40 tickets per meal at a cost of forty cents. The cafeteria moved to the Home Economics Administration Building, now Stone Hall, when it opened in 1957. Thanks to the leadership and fortitude of Mary, the home economics program had come a long way since its days in drafty, decrepit Ladies Hall.

In a 1995 interview, Professor Emeritus Janalyce Rouls said, "When I was a small child my mother came to Purdue with the extension home economics club people, and it was the year that Matthews Hall was dedicated. We were kind of appalled that she would leave us to go to Purdue for a night or two, but she came home filled with the spirit of Purdue and education for women."

In 1926, the School of Home Economics was established and Mary Matthews was appointed the first dean. Home economics was no longer in the School of Science. It had come into its own through Mary's guidance. The school was organized into five departments: applied design, clothing and textiles, foods and nutrition, home administration, and institutional management. Mary was a professor of home economics and head of the Department of Home Administration. There were 368 undergraduate students and three graduate students enrolled.

Mary attended the Home Management House Conference in March of 1926, held at Teachers College, Columbia University, New York City. The "Foreword" in the conference booklet was written by Professor Emma H. Gunther, organizer. She stated, "The term 'practice house' does not do justice to the larger concept of a home that will be an inspiration as well as a workable demonstration. . . . to bring about a new conception of the art of living—this is the attainable ideal of the Home Management House."

Gunther ended her piece with a commentary on how the latest domestic advances had affected women's lives in 1926. Her words could have been written today: "We have universalized the machine as a servant. If this has increased the pace of life, it has at least saved us from the routine of drudgery. All this concern about time schedules is only by way of attaining a higher end. The ultimate purpose is to save the homemaker the time and energy needed for more expressive living."

The conference covered "Home Management House Functioning," which included time studies of household operations. The book states, "By observing methods of performing one piece of routine work, the most economical method in time, expense, and energy can be deduced, and this should then become the standard method of performing that particular process." One of a few household operations covered in the booklet was ironing twelve, twenty-one-inch napkins. A "process chart" outlined the steps in ironing the napkins with "improvised equipment," which was an ironing board obtained from a closet fifteen feet away, and the "standard equipment," which was an ironing board built into a wall with iron and other needs contained there. The summary of the completed study concluded that the improvised equipment took 110 motions while the standard equipment took seventy-three. Total time per week to iron twelve napkins with the improvised method was eight minutes and six and a half seconds, and the total time for the standard method was four minutes and thirty-nine seconds. If a woman used a standard built-into-the-wall ironing board, she would save a total time per year of three hours, forty-nine minutes, and thirty-two seconds when ironing twelve napkins per week.

The conference booklet also covered time/motion/fatigue studies on weekly changing and making of beds and reducing walking distances in dishwashing. The bed-making study included a bibliography that cited several publications by Lillian and Frank Gilbreth. Lillian was an inventor, engineer, and industrial psychologist who was known as the "mother of modern management" for her work with her husband on pioneering industrial management techniques. She was one of the first "superwomen" to manage both family and career, and eventually, she would be invited to teach at Purdue. Lillian was a mother of twelve children born over a span of seventeen years. Two of her children cowrote the 1946 novel *Cheaper by the Dozen*, based on a humorous look at the highly organized life of the Gilbreth household. The book was made into a movie in 1950 with a remake in 2003 that veered from the storyline of the book.

Lillian was passionate about finding efficient and productive ways to perform every task—from washing dishes to brushing teeth. Together, the Gilbreths outlined their management style in several books. Sadly, none of these studies listed Lillian as coauthor because their publicist believed a book's credibility would suffer if readers knew a woman was involved. After her husband's death in 1924, two years before the Home Management House Conference that Mary Matthews attended, she continued her career as an inventor, industrial engineer, and industrial psychologist while raising her large family. Gilbreth helped General Electric Company and other prominent companies by assisting in the improvement of the designs of many kitchen appliances, including the electric food mixer and a trash can with a foot-pedal lid-opener. Lillian was named the first female member of the American Society of Mechanical Engineers in 1926.

In 1935, Lillian became a full professor in the School of Industrial Engineering at Purdue University. President Edward Elliott hired Lillian with the intention of "introducing new forces for the . . . effective education of young women." Lillian lived on campus in the women's residence halls during her time at Purdue, and helped improve the motion study labs on campus, making them more accessible to the local agricultural industry.

A story in the Home Management House Conference booklet written by Lillian entitled "Fatigue in Industry and the Home" said, "The fatigue problem is very similar in industry and in the home, for home keeping is housekeeping plus, and housekeeping is an industrial process."

Her final thoughts were ones to which women today may relate:

> The problems of physical fatigue are less serious every day, as power and machines make heavy physical work a decreasing part of home keeping. But the problems of psychological fatigue are increasing in importance. Worry, pressure, friction, clutter, monotony—these are some of the underlying causes of this psychological fatigue. . . . When we have transferred efficient practice from industry, and made housekeeping a science, we shall have more time and interest for the art of homemaking.

This was the year three more Home Management Houses were created at Purdue. Conceivably, Mary attended the conference to learn new ideas to implement in her Home Management Houses. Mary is to be commended for her many accomplishments, which included educating women and men and leading Purdue's School of Home Economics, but perhaps she should be most commended for something she did *not* do. She did not establish a "practice baby."

One topic that was covered at the conference, but that Mary did not implement at a Purdue Home Management House, was the inclusion of a "practice baby." Many Home Management Houses at other universities had a resident baby that was the center of the household. May C. Ney of Buffalo College for Teachers wrote an article in the conference booklet entitled "The Child in the Home Management House." She stated, "I'm convinced that the baby does more to draw the girls together into a real family group than any other factor in the practice house life. Perhaps there are two questions uppermost in our minds when we think of the baby in the practice house. 'What do the girls gain from the experience which carries over?' and 'Is it fair to the baby?'"

A senior girl, the "practice mother," was put in complete charge of the baby and kept careful records of his or her development and did the baby's laundry for a thirty-day period. After her practice time was complete, another student took on the role of practice mother for her thirty-day requirement. In essence, the practice baby had a new "mother" every month. One of the university's teachers in psychology came to the house every two months to observe the baby and determine if he or she was on track developmentally.

The practice babies were loaned on contract for a year or more by local orphanages and child welfare organizations. Eventually, they were returned to their orphanages for adoption. Cornell University began incorporating practice babies into the curriculum in 1919 with the first baby named Dicky Domecon (pronounced "Dough-me-con," a Frankenstein-ish word morphing together "domestic" and "economics"). Prospective adoptive parents desired Domecon babies because they had been raised according to the "most up-to-date scientific principles." The practice mothers kept scrapbooks with photographs of the baby's milestones. Practice babies often came to the house ill or undernourished and left healthy—at least physically.

As time passed, research in early childhood development pointed to the need for a baby to have a primary bond with a single caregiver. It was not until 1954 that child welfare officials at the Illinois Department of Public Welfare became concerned and deemed the practice house not a "normal setting" for a baby. Babette Penner, director of the Women's Service Division of United Charities, said, "Imagine what anxieties there are in a child who is given a bottle in twelve or more pairs of arms."

Imagine, indeed. Today the idea seems barbaric. For women who know the ardent tug of motherhood, the thought of a practice baby nurtured for just thirty days and then passed to another woman like a dessert tray sends an ache to the heart.

Mary L. Matthews sits in the living room of one of the Practice Houses on the Purdue University campus in January 1951, the year before she retired as dean of the School of Home Economics. Matthews debuted the Practice House concept in 1919 to provide a hands-on environment for the home economics student to practice what she had been taught in the classroom. Courtesy of Purdue University Libraries, Archives and Special Collections.

The Home Management Houses continued to be part of the home economics curriculum at Purdue until 1983. Beginning in the 1940s, Professor Mary Louise Foster was a supervisor in the Practice House located on Waldron. "The budget was skin and bones," remembers Foster, age eighty-seven in 2010. Foster was a supervisor until Practice Houses were dropped from the Purdue curriculum. Many students dreaded their time in the Practice House. They had to move out of their dorm or sorority for six to eight weeks, and they did not like leaving their friends and daily college lives. In addition, it was an added expense, for the students continued to pay their residential costs along with a fee at the Practice House. Professors, on the other hand, liked the concept of Home Management Houses. According to

Foster, whatever Mary Matthews advised, the professors backed her idea. "They trusted her," explained Foster. "She was a very intelligent woman. You didn't question her."

Mary had a very good relationship with various retailers, particularly Sears, Roebuck, and Co., which donated household equipment like stoves, washers, dryers, and sewing machines for use in the Home Management Houses and the classrooms.

An article in the *Indianapolis Star* dated Sunday, March 17, 1968 featured Purdue's Home Management Houses. Some young women were married with children while going to school, but they still spent time at a Home Management House. The article states, "Mrs. Harold Hammond of English [Indiana], the only married student, says: 'I've learned so much I never knew really how to organize and plan well. I know I'll be more efficient when I'm home and will run a smoother house and have more time for my children. They are doing well. They are accustomed to a changing school and living situation. Both my husband and I have been in school all of their lives. It's a way of life for them.'"

Foster was quoted in the article with her prediction of the future: "Studies indicate that young women of this age group will have household help a good many years of their married lives. They will not only be the homemaker, but will also be a wage earner, away from home and finding it necessary to employ someone to follow their directions for caring for their homes."

Eventually, social changes in the lives of women made the practice house a domestic dinosaur. The ideology in the School of Home Economics changed in favor of hard science over practical applications. Some teachings of the Practice House are relevant today, like adhering to a budget and saving steps with every task through motion and time studies; however, much of what was taught, like ironing napkins, laundering doilies, and making creamed salmon on toast, seems laughable today.

Whirlwind for Women

By 1915, Lella was off and running as a pioneer home demonstration agent traveling Indiana by train, horse, buggy, and occasionally automobile (or "machine," as she and Kate referred to cars). Often in rural areas, the dirt roads were almost impassable even to a horse and buggy, but farm women needed Lella and the county agents she hired, so she persevered in all kinds of road conditions. Many times she arrived home in the wee hours of the morning, say 3:00 a.m., only to leave again at 9:00 a.m. The job was perfect for her energetic, quick-witted personality. She must have enjoyed the challenge of changing women's lives by bringing the teachings of Purdue University into their farm kitchens, vegetable gardens, and sewing baskets.

Purdue Dean Emeritus Earl Butz, who was former Secretary of Agriculture under the administrations of Richard Nixon and Gerald Ford, said in a 1995 interview, "Miss Gaddis was a practical soul who organized extension and got the home agents out in the counties, who was a fighter for home economics extension. She was a pioneer. She cleared the way for people to come. She set the path."

Standards for homemade products such as butter needed to be improved. Teaching women to follow recipes and measure when cooking and baking helped advance quality and nutrition. Displays at county fairs and contests also helped raise the bar in food preparation and preservation, clothing construction, and numerous other house-hold and farm chores. When farm women met as a group and learned more about domestic and farm advancements, the health of their families improved, some of their burdens were lightened, and they garnered much-needed social time and support. Some homes were used for "result-demonstrations," where groups of women came to see progress made. Water systems were innovations as were the methods of installing them in homes without electricity. Elevated tanks were filled by windmill power. Lella made speeches and gave talks to such groups as a "thimble club," which is a sewing group that commonly made quilts. Kate waited at home and often referred to her loneliness in her diaries.

One of Lella's first stops was in Wells County where she gave the first demonstration on cold pack canning in a neighborhood yard under the shade of an oak tree. She used an oil stove, a wash boiler with boards in the bottom on which to place the cans to keep them from breaking when the water boiled, and a bounty of fresh green beans and peas to preserve through the three-hour process. Kate writes:

> February 3: Lella gone all this week. She sure will know the state and I will too as I have to look up often.

> February 17: Am still lonesome. Such a big baby.

> June 24: Lella makes a speech and I do hear cover herself with glory at Purdue, I do hear.

The sisters' finances were looking up, and Lella received a $200 raise that year. They immediately invested the additional income, as Kate records on May 1, "We get three shares in the Purdue Bank for $375 today."

They also used their newfound financial freedom to take a trip. With their friend Anna Roberta McNeill ("Mack"), the trio headed out West to see the Panama-Pacific Exposition in San Francisco with a stop along the way at the Panama-California Exposition in San Di-ego. Both exhibitions were akin to a World's Fair and were held in celebration of the opening of the Panama Canal, but San Francisco also highlighted the recovery from the city's 1906 earthquake. Kate writes on June 23, "Am busy as a cranberry merchant getting ready to go to San Francisco. Can hardly believe it."

The idiom "busy as a cranberry merchant" was one both Lella and Kate uttered when their to-do lists were long. The complete saying is "busy as a cranberry merchant at Thanksgiving," but the women abbreviated the expression. Busy they were, sending telegrams to secure their train tickets and itinerary, making out their wills, and obtaining "traveler's cheques." It is not clear which woman planned the schedule that included many stops and visits with numerous friends and family. However, it was most likely Lella. She was the organizer, the traveler, the woman who got things done, and she made quick and accurate decisions.

They started for California from Lafayette's Big-Four Depot. In her diary, Kate recorded what she saw out the train window (snow-capped mountains) and commented on her accommodations: "Nice and clean when you travel first-class Pullman." On the way out, they met up with their friend Mack's aunts who lived in Denver, and the aunts joined the Hoosier women on the journey. They traveled on to Colorado Springs, and from there they boarded the train for Salt Lake City, Utah. Kate's handwriting appears shaky. The train's chug-chugging along caused her perfect schoolteacher cursive to take a beating. She writes on July 5 of the journey, "Pass through Royal Gorge. Perfectly wonderful, on the Rio Grand Railroad. Perfectly beautiful. Pass the Great Divide in the night."

The women attended a concert for the governor of Georgia at the Mormon Tabernacle. Then they were off to California. On July 7, Kate records, "Nothing but sagebrush and cactus for hundreds and hundreds of miles. Why do people want to live in this forsaken country?"

Once in California, they visited Lella and Kate's Aunt Margaret Campbell and made a stop in Los Angeles before heading to San Diego. Kate writes on July 9, "Went out to see the exhibition grounds. They are beautiful. Staid [sic] at the San Diego Hotel."

The women spent a short time at the Panama-California Exposition in San Diego, which was located in Balboa Park, today an important cultural center housing major museums. The exposition was held from 1915 to 1917 and led to the world-famous San Diego Zoo that began with the abandoned exotic animals from the exhibition.

Next, Lella, Kate, Mack, and their traveling companions were off to San Francisco where they took a sightseeing tour of Golden Gate Park (the bridge would not be built until 1937), China Town, and the "fisheries." It was their first time to see an ocean. Kate writes:

> July 13: The girls took a dip in the ocean this p.m.
>
> July 14: Went out to the Expo. The Canadian building is lovely. The Indiana building very fine. Heard [John Philip] Sousa Band. The flowers are beautiful, but I like San Diego better.

The next leg of the Gaddis sister's trip was by steamer ship. They boarded a boat for Portland, Oregon, and on July 15, Kate records, "On the Great Northern. Such a beautiful, big steamer. We are all seasick. Lella and Mack do not miss a meal. Over 600 on board. Only 150 able for dinner tonight. "

Along the way, the women met up with various friends and relatives. They visited Portland, Seattle, and then Mack's Canadian homeland. By another boat, they reached Vancouver and proceeded to Lake Louise and Winnipeg where they visited the University of Manitoba's School of Agriculture. Kate said they had "such fine buildings." For three women from Indiana, and especially homebody Kate, traveling across the country for a month-long journey in the 1910s was a monumental excursion. They head home on July 27, arriving in Chicago two days later, where they spend time shopping at Marshall Field's before boarding the train to Lafayette. Kate writes of the trip's expense on July 30, "Count up and see our trip cost me $235 and we did everything we wanted to."

In the back of her diary, Kate kept a running list of "Meals on trip out west 1915." Her most expensive meal was a lunch for eighty-five cents. Her least expensive meal was breakfast at just a quarter. She also kept a running account of the miles they traveled between stops. The total traveled was 4,888 miles. Another page lists the "Sleepers" they traveled in and the costs. The least expensive railroad sleeper car they traveled in cost $1. The most expensive sleeper car was on their return jaunt from Vancouver to Chicago at $13.

❧ ❧

The year 1916 began with Lella and Kate paying a visit to Mary Matthews on January 2, and the next day Mary ate supper at the Gaddis home. This year's diary is different in appearance from the others. The cover is black textured fabric rather than leather; the pages are edged in a marbleized red and yellow. Kate wrote about house plans and visits to potential housing lots. They had their house on Salisbury wired for electricity, assumedly to make it more marketable to sell. It cost the sisters $44 for the wiring and $27.65 for the fixtures that would replace the gaslights. She said that during the wiring, they had to "jump cracks in the floor," and it would "be mighty nice when all done." She continued:

> March 15: Have the lights but no meter so I burn and have a good time all by myself.
>
> March 16: Have the meter so we are a little careful about snapping.

Kate was freewheeling with the electricity when she knew she had no meter, racking up an electric bill. Once the meter was installed she said they were careful about "snapping." The push button wall switches used back then made a distinctive "snap" when pressed.

On March 10, Kate writes, "We went out to Russell Street and look at lots. We think it is so pretty out there." Lella and Kate purchased lot 21 on Russell Street in West Lafayette for $1,000 cash. Then they took bids from contractors to begin building their new home. Kate was the one who met with most of the workers because Lella was traveling for her extension effort. The women must have received a government loan to build their house, for Kate noted, "Sammie is going to furnish all the money we want." "Sammie" was a slang term for Uncle Sam.

For the next three months, Kate recorded each step in the building of their new home from pouring the foundation and plastering the walls to installation of flooring and packing for the move. The total cost was $5,665. Their new home had a sleeping porch, which was common at the time. Often upstairs, a sleeping porch is a room with open sides or many windows to permit sleeping in the open air. Many people believed that fresh air helped sufferers of tuberculosis, the leading cause of death at the turn of the twentieth century. Health experts then also touted the benefits of fresh air for avoiding other illnesses. Before the advent of air conditioning, people slept on sleeping porches in the summer months to keep cool. Yet later, even in February, Kate commented that they were still spending the night on their sleeping porch.

Along with her record of the construction of their house, Kate interspersed sentences about every town and event to which Lella traveled during that time. She writes:

> July 3: Lella went to Middle Burrow to make a Fourth of July speech.
>
> July 20: The bull in the china shop helped move. Had our lunch in the new house.
>
> July 21: Finish moving. Margaret Christie our first guest.

Lella and Kate were so proud of their new home that they invited photographer J. C. Allen to visit the next year and take pictures of the completed house. Allen was a renowned photographer who captured rural and farm life from the early 1900s to the late 1960s. He rendered in black and white photographs the emotion and historical significance of farm living, from milk cows, tractors, and barns, to farmers working the land, mothers baking bread, and children playing in cornfields. In addition, he was a photographer for Purdue University, and today there is an extensive collection of his work in the Purdue University Virginia Kelly Karnes Archives and Special Collections Research Center. John O. Allen, third generation photographer, still maintains a studio and archives in West Lafayette, Indiana.

❧

The remainder of 1916 was smattered with epic events, both personal and worldly. Purdue hosted an Indiana Centennial celebration on

October 31, and Kate's school was dismissed early so that teachers and children could attend. Purdue combined the celebration of Indiana's 100th year with the commemoration of founder John Purdue's birthday, which was on October 31, 1802. President Woodrow Wilson was elected, and on November 20, Lella and Kate's grandmother, Mary Smith Gaddis, turned one hundred years old—an astonishing milestone in 1916. Grandmother Gaddis celebrated her centennial the same year as the state of Indiana. Kate devoted five pages in the back of her diary to write about the birthday celebration for her grandmother. It was held at the Gaddis sisters' new home with fifty guests for dinner and a cake with one hundred candles. Grandmother Gaddis wore a black silk dress that was given to her by Lella and Kate the previous Christmas.

On January 1, 1917, Kate wrote that she thought she would not keep a diary that year, but decided to after all. It is curious, for the diary looks the most worn of all the journals handed down to her great-niece Miriam Epple-Heath. The spine is missing leather and the edges are worn raw. The light blue shoebox that houses the collection of diaries once held a pair of nurse's shoes. The lid bears an image of a nurse and copy that reads, "The Clinic Shoe for young women in white. Nothing could be finer." Throughout her diaries, Kate talks of buying new shoes; some she returned because they did not feel right. She battled aching feet, which was probably a symptom of poor circulation brought on by diabetes.

This year, the Indiana Home Economics Association (IHEA) with Mary Matthews as president held a contest for the 4-H Bread and Canning Clubs. The winners were awarded a trip to Washington, DC. Agatha Conner, age thirteen, baked 403 loaves of bread, and Ruby Smith, age seventeen, canned 320 quarts of fruits and vegetables. Lella chaperoned the girls on their winning trip. Fleischman Yeast contributed $10 of the $123.25 given by the association for the journey. From Kate's record on January 20, it sounds as if the trip took Lella and the young "misses" to high places: "Lella gets home 7:35. Having shook hands with the President."

The United States was on the cusp of entering World War I, and Kate sounded concerned yet comforted by President Woodrow Wilson. Wilson was waging battles abroad and at home. Since his first presidential campaign, American women had been staging suffrage marches and demonstrations and going to jail to urge the president and legislature to give them the right to vote. Women marched around the White House during both of his inaugural ceremonies in 1913 and 1917. Some battles for woman suffrage were won state-by-state. Kate writes:

> February 22: The Legislature passed the bill and Indiana women get to vote. Me for voting.
>
> April 3: We really are at war with Germany. Seems terrible but we were dragged into it. Wilson [the president of the U.S.] made a wonderful speech before congress yesterday.

Indiana women were granted the right to vote in presidential elections only. Full voting rights would not be realized until 1920. In opposition, there was an anti-suffrage movement, which argued that most women really did not want to vote, and they were probably not qualified to exercise the right anyway. Some suffragists used humor to counter such arguments. Famous writer Alice Duer Miller wrote a column "Are Women People?" later titled "Women are People!" for the *New York Tribune*. She wrote this satirical list for the National American Woman Suffrage Association in 1915, which was made into a poster entitled "Why We Oppose Votes For Men":

> 1. Because man's place is in the army.
>
> 2. Because no really manly man wants to settle any question otherwise than by fighting about it.
>
> 3. Because if men should adopt peacable [sic] methods women will no longer look up to them.
>
> 4. Because men will lose their charm if they step out of their natural sphere and interest themselves in other matters than feats of arms, uniforms and drums.

5. Because men are too emotional to vote. Their conduct at baseball games and political conventions shows this, while their innate tendency to appeal to force renders them particularly unfit for the task of government.

Once World War I was declared, life changed for the Gaddis family in many ways. Kate and Mack knitted for the American Red Cross at meetings held in Ladies Hall. In the summer of 1917, the Red Cross put out an urgent call for knitted goods to help fight the war. The need was one and a half million each of knitted wristlets, mufflers, sweaters, and pairs of socks. Soldiers were in dire need of socks, for they spent weeks or months entrenched in wet and freezing conditions. The Red Cross provided yarn and instructions. "Knit for Sammie!" was the rallying cry of the knitters. American soldiers were called "Sammies," short for Uncle Sam. Promotional posters bore the slogan "Knit your bit." In the back of her 1917 diary, Kate listed what she made for the war effort during a six-month period. She knitted twelve pairs of socks, four pairs of wristlets, and one helmet. A wristlet was a knitted sleeve with a hole for the thumb and an opening for all four fingers. The wristlet kept the palm and wrist warm while allowing the soldiers to use their fingers when handling a gun or bayonet. The helmet was not like a helmet we think of today, but a knit stocking cap that came down the neck (like the top of a turtleneck sweater) and covered the sides of the head. Just the face was exposed.

After the United States entered the war, the newly established Agricultural Extension Service quickly became a catalyst for the nation to attain wartime goals. The central goal was to increase the nation's production of food, particularly wheat. Yet men were leaving farms to join the armed services or to work in war industries. Purdue's Agricultural Extension Service was needed more than ever to help the country by helping Indiana's farm people.

Because of the war effort, George Christie, director of the Department of Agricultural Extension (whom Kate calls "G.I."), had a new position, and Lella received word about changes in her job. Kate records:

April 11: G.I. has been appointed State Food Hustler or something of the sort.

August 10: The Food Bill has gone through and Lella is to
have her new job.

August 11: Lella is to have a salary of $1600 with a fixed sum
for traveling expenses which is not at all small besides she
had 5 institutes at $5 per.

"State Food Hustler" was Kate's term for Christie's state food director
position that would require him to "hustle" more food from Indiana
farms. The bill she referred to was one of two major laws Congress
passed relating to food and agriculture, the Food and Fuel Control
Act and the Food Production Act. President Woodrow Wilson signed
both into law on August 10, 1917. The Food and Fuel Control Act
authorized the president to set up a Food Administration, headed by
Herbert Hoover, which would control the handling and distribution
of food. The Food Production Act gave the Department of Agriculture
responsibility for encouraging the production of commodities, as well
as moving them to market and conserving perishable products by canning, drying, and preserving. The county agent was called upon to
work for both agencies. An emergency appropriation of more than
four million dollars was provided for "the further development of the
Extension Service." The Purdue Agricultural Extension Service was
buzzing with what was to happen next as the staff would aid their
country by educating the Indiana farmer, his wife, and children. Lella
had her work cut out for her to help Indiana's rural women. If anyone
was ready, she was. Kate writes on September 25, "Lella is busy getting
things in order. Her new job is a fine one, but we don't intend to let
it turn our heads."

❧

The year was fraught with anxiety as the war hit on a personal front
for the Gaddis sisters when their adored nephew, Paul Riley, who lived
with them while attending Purdue, was called to enlist soon after his
graduation. At the same time, Lella was occupied with reorganizing
her extension efforts to do her part to increase food production and
assist farm women in learning food conservation and preservation.
Kate writes:

> June 5: This is Conscription Day and 10,000,000 men between 21-31 register. Paul came in here and registered.
>
> July 19: Tomorrow is the conscription and there are many anxious hearts.
>
> July 20: Today is the conscription and Paul is among the first drawn.

Conscription was the term used for the draft or selective service. By August, Paul was in Officer Training Camp at Fort Benjamin Harrison in Indianapolis, Indiana. In November, he was made first lieutenant. Before he left for Fort Travis in Texas, he married his girl, Ruth Sayers. Kate writes bittersweetly:

> November 28: This is Sonny's wedding day and a very simple, pretty wedding it is.
>
> December 12: Ruth and Paul come tonight from Boswell. They do not get here until quite late. We went to bed and left them play cribbage. My, but we hate to see the laddy leave tomorrow.
>
> December 13: Paul left at 7:49 this morning for Camp Travis at Ft. Huston, Texas.

Paul was in the Signal Corp pilot training at Kelly Field, San Antonio, Texas. He would receive his wings with as little as six to twelve hours of flight training. Planes were not armed with mounted guns back then, and there were no parachutes. Pilots used handguns as they flew at three thousand feet altitude. After Paul received his wings, he was assigned to the 48th Aerial Squadron at Mitchell Field, Long Island, New York, in May 1918.

The events of 1917 unfurled: the war was on; Lella had a new, thrilling position with a pay raise; the sisters' nephew graduated from Purdue, married, and went off to war right before Christmas; Kate knitted for the cause; and she began her twenty-ninth year of teaching. However, by mid-October, she was sick: "Lella brought me out to the sanatorium this morning. I had dinner and was looked over by a doc. and then given a nice clean bath".

The Wabash Valley Sanitarium was established in 1906 to specialize in hydrotherapy, or what they called "water cure," and the dietary regimens that were popular then. Some years later, it became a hospital for the care and treatment of nervous and mental illness. The brick Victorian building with a wraparound veranda was set on beautiful, wooded grounds on what is today North River Road across from the Wabash River in West Lafayette. Prior to her admittance, Kate mentioned that she was "so lame" she could "hardly walk," and the doctor thought she had rheumatism. Kate records:

> October 21: Busy again with 2 baths. On a diet of mostly bran things. This is a nice quiet place and they are so kind and nice.

> October 22: Time doesn't hang on your hands here. Too many baths for that.

> October 23: I think I have had all the chaff and fruit I can stand.

> October 29: Having all kinds of baths now. They surely do get you nice and clean.

Kate stayed in the sanatorium for two weeks, and she faithfully wrote in the diary she had considered foregoing at the beginning of the year. She had many visitors including the Christies and of course Lella and Mack. It must have been hard on Lella to be concerned about her sister as she began her new venture with extension's war effort and continued her travels across the state. Lella worried about Kate and her health. Kate worried about Lella and her travels in all kinds of weather conditions. They were both working women, juggling family needs and schedules, just like women today.

Wheat will Win the War

The rally cry was "Food will win the war! Don't waste it!" The American government emphasized that the country whose food was best conserved would be the victor in World War I. In *Foods That Will Win The War And How To Cook Them* by C. Houston and Alberta M. Goudiss, published in 1918, it warned, "Waste in your kitchen means starvation in some other kitchen across the sea. Our Allies are asking for 450,000,000 bushels of wheat, and we are told that even then theirs will be a privation (small) loaf. Crop shortage and unusual demand has left Canada and the United States, which are the largest sources of wheat, with but 300,000,000 bushels available to export. The deficit must be met by reducing consumption on this side of the Atlantic."

President Woodrow Wilson said, "To provide adequate supplies for the coming year is of absolutely vital importance to the conduct of the war, and without a very conscientious elimination of waste and very strict economy in our food consumption, we cannot hope to fulfill this primary duty."

Lella Gaddis's job description as the state leader of home demonstration now included hiring emergency agents to help the state's women learn how to conserve food and "serve the cause of freedom." The U.S. Food Administration, headed by Herbert Hoover, produced posters with the bold headline "SAVE" and a list of the essential foods to conserve:

1. Wheat—use more corn.

2. Meat—use more fish & beans.

3. Fats—use just enough.

4. Sugar—use syrups.

The Food Administration also emphasized six points regarding "FOOD":

1. Buy it with thought.

2. Cook it with care.

3. Serve just enough.

4. Save what will keep.

5. Eat what would spoil.

6. Home-grown is best.

Another U.S. Food Administration poster promoted the saving of fat: "Fats are fuel for fighters. Bake, boil and broil more—fry less."

Some posters appealed to the emotions of the country's immigrants with the words, "You came here seeking freedom, you must now help to preserve it. Wheat is needed for the allies. Waste nothing."

After the Food Production Act provided an emergency appropriation for the further development of the extension service, there were more than sixteen hundred emergency agents, including six hundred women, across the nation. The war brought the agents together in a common goal that transformed their individual efforts into a unified national agenda. Their work brought them prestige and increased their morale. They were seen as the patriotic leaders of much-needed war campaigns. The first responsibility of the county agent was to

In 1918, Lella Gaddis, age forty-one, traveled Indiana clutching her home demonstration case, visiting rural women to teach them how to conserve food and "serve the cause of freedom" during World War I. Courtesy of Purdue University Libraries, Archives and Special Collections.

campaign for increases in production, particularly with regard to wheat crops. Other campaigns were carried out to increase the production of corn, oats, barley, and rye. Pork, mutton, poultry, and egg production campaigns were also touted. While the farmer increased production, the farmer's wife decreased consumption in the home.

President Wilson issued a proclamation calling Americans to display their patriotism by following voluntary "meatless Tuesdays," "sweetless Saturdays," and "wheatless Wednesdays and Mondays." Tuesdays and Saturdays were "porkless." The cutting of waste and substituting plentiful ingredients for scarce became known as "Hooverizing." Herbert Hoover emphasized that the call for conservation was voluntary and rested on the "goodwill of, and the willingness to sacrifice by, the American people." Yet he also said, "We have but one police force—the American Woman—and we depend upon her to organize in co-operation with our state and local Food Administrators to see that these rules are obeyed by that small minority who may fail."

In essence, Hoover was telling women to monitor their sister homemakers and by "peer pressure" encourage all to comply with the effort to conserve food. In large part on the home front, winning the war was in the hands of the women who purchased the food staples, tended the gardens, preserved the fare, baked the bread, and cooked the meals. If the farm men increased production of crops and meat, yet the women prepared the food in a wasteful manner, all efforts would be futile. There were no factories for the mass baking of bread, canning of vegetables, or butchering of cattle and hogs. Food was produced and preserved on the farm. Soldiers needed food to fight. The farmer and the women of America were called to win the war, and Lella Gaddis and her hires would educate and motivate the women of Indiana to do just that.

Ironically, the promotion to eat less meat, fats, and sugar is similar to the healthy dietary guidelines of today suggested by the U.S. Department of Health and Human Services. Without knowing it, in 1918, as Americans cut back on these staples and ate from their home gardens (which today we call "organic"), they were eating a diet rich in fruits, vegetables, and grains and low in fat, much like the dietary guidelines of the present day.

Under Lella's leadership, there was cooperation between home economics and other extension departments. Lella explained, "An example of the joint educational efforts of the Extension Service was the need during the war years to encourage farmers to grow more wheat. A new strain of wheat was being demonstrated by Soils and Crops. Home Ec demonstrated bread making throughout Indiana at this time to interest women in the wheat. Another example, we worked very hard along with the men to get safer milk supplies for families."

The "milk campaign" resulted in herds of Indiana dairy cattle freed from tuberculosis and brucellosis, cattle diseases that had been causes of tuberculosis and undulant fever in humans. Leaders in Agricultural Extension supported laws that enforced safe milk supplies for millions of people in Indiana through campaigns that were met with opposition from dairy farmers who saw the laws as forcing higher costs to them, even though the result was the assurance of safe food.

Lella and her agents held demonstrations promoting "Liberty Gardens." War gardens grew all over the state because "homegrown was best" for the war effort. Railroad companies called on their employees to cultivate vacant lots along their rights-of-way, furnishing the land free or for a nominal rental. Often the companies supplied seeds and helped prepare the soil. Posters were displayed in train stations, and the railroads distributed gardening manuals produced by the War Garden Commission. Gardens were an important factor in relieving the demands on the trains, allowing them to carry more commercial freight. If food was grown at home, less was delivered across the country. "Grow food! Use all vacant lots! Work to win!" American women and their children were determined in the noble venture of the war garden, and Lella and her staff were teachers and cheerleaders.

They also taught canning and preserving with a minimum of sugar and the art of drying foods as preservation. They instituted campaigns that included demonstrations for both quick and yeast breads. First 50-50 breads (half white flour and half wheat flour), then 25-75, and finally the all-substitute breads were taught to women who were very receptive to the idea. A special campaign demonstrated how potatoes could replace flour and resulted in delicious potato bread, rolls, and more served on Indiana dinner tables.

In communities where there was a scarcity of vegetable garden seeds, extension agents arranged an exchange between counties. There was an "eat more fish" campaign to enable beef, pork, and chicken to be sent to the fighting forces. This was when cottage cheese came to be a popular staple in American homes. To free cheddar and other cheese products for the war effort and cut down on meat consumption, a cottage cheese project was instituted. The home extension agents gave demonstrations on how to save skim milk by making good cottage cheese. A poster of the time read, "Eat More Cottage Cheese . . . You'll Need Less Meat . . . A Postal Card Will Bring Recipes . . . Cottage Cheese or Meat? Ask Your Pocketbook!" Americans changed the name to cottage cheese from the German name, "schmear kase." Dairy processors saw cottage cheese as a new marketable product, and they liked that it was profitable. Thus, today in America, cottage cheese is a common side dish.

Conserving food and using every drop and morsel was moralized across the country. Lella and her agents preached the gospel of frugality in the kitchen. Waste was a no-no, and the authors of *Foods That Will Win The War And How To Cook Them* wrote some strong words on the subject:

> According to a well-known domestic scientist, the only things which should find their way to the garbage pail are:

> • Egg shells—after being used to clear coffee

> • Potato skins—after having been cooked on the potato.

> • Banana skins—if there are no tan shoes to be cleaned.

> • Bones—after having been boiled in soup kettle.

> • Coffee grounds—if there is no garden where they can be used for fertilizer, or if they are not desired as filling for pin-cushions.

> • Tea leaves—after every tea serving, if they are not needed for brightening carpets or rugs when swept.

> • Asparagus ends—after being cooked and drained for soup.

> • Spinach, etc.—decayed leaves and dirty ends of roots.

The authors continued with a final stab at the heart of a woman's domestic and American identity: "If more than this is now thrown away, you are wasting the family income and not fulfilling your part in the great world struggle. . . . The art of utilizing the leftovers is an important factor in this prevention of waste. The thrifty have always known it. The careless have always ignored it. But now as a measure of home economy as well as a patriotic service, the leftover must be handled intelligently."

Mary Matthews also encouraged food conservation through her Department of Household Economics, and she was named to three impressive governmental entities. She was made director of home economics for the Indiana Food Administration, and chairman of the Home Economics Committee under the Indiana State Council of

Defense. She held the only federal commission in Indiana that was issued to a woman. Mary created numerous bulletins that were widely distributed to help homemakers with the substitutions of foods.

Many cookbooks of the time offered recipes that conserved wheat, meats, fats, and sugar. Below is a recipe for a cake that conserved all four foods, yet was nutritious. It is taken from *Foods That Will Win The War And How To Cook Them* (1918):

Wheatless, Eggless, Butterless, Milkless, Sugarless Cake
1 cup corn syrup
2 cups water
2 cups raisins
2 tablespoons fat
1 teaspoon salt
2 teaspoons cinnamon
1 teaspoon nutmeg
1 ½ cups fine cornmeal, 2 cups rye flour;
    or 3 ½ cups whole wheat flour
1 ½ teaspoons baking powder, or, ½ teaspoon soda

Cook corn syrup, water, raisins, fat, salt, and spices slowly 15 minutes. When cool, add flour, soda, or baking powder, thoroughly blended. Bake in slow oven 1 hour. The longer this cake is kept, the better the texture and flavor. This recipe is sufficient to fill one medium-sized bread pan.

Farmers were in a double bind as they attempted to increase production at the same time men were leaving the farm to go into the armed forces or work in war industries in cities. Extension agents helped solve the problem of the shortage of farm workers by organizing and placing women in the Woman's Land Army of America (WLAA). The WLAA was established in April of 1918 to train women to work in agricultural jobs vacated by men serving in the military. The women were paid for their work on public or private farms. The *Handbook of*

Standards for the Woman's Land Army of America discussed the various aspects of women working on a farm including the kinds of labor, wages, camp organization, and uniforms. The handbook stated, "Women should not attempt to do farm work hampered by skirts or by clothing which constricts the muscles. A uniform carefully designed to meet the needs of the woman land worker has been adopted by the National Board of the Woman's Land Army and can be supplied on application." The farm gear women wore became known as "coveralls," also known as "womanalls" or "freedomalls."

The handbook also discussed "individual placement" and referred to the safety of the woman on the farm. It is obvious that there was concern about the need of a female chaperone to accompany all women to avoid any "hanky-panky." The handbook declared, "No women should be placed singly on farms unless their welfare can be satisfactorily safeguarded, and unless there is a woman in the farmer's household." An agreement that covered all aspects of the woman's employment was included in the handbook.

Both Mary Matthews and Lella Gaddis signed a report for the year ending June 30, 1918, summing up the patriotic efforts of Indiana homemakers under the leadership of home economics extension. The report conveyed the two women's common goal "to make the best use of foods, so that our men at war and those of our allies might be sustained." Mary and Lella were united in a shared objective for the war effort, their country, and the women of Indiana.

Lella said of her wartime position, "The food demands of the allies and of our army, and the scarcity of labor on the farm, have intensified the work of the Home Demonstration Agent." This was an understatement, for the work of the home demonstration agent during World War I intensified each day to the point of exhaustion.

꧁꧂

Kate's 1918 diary contains references to the various ways she helped in the war effort. On several occasions, she went to the courthouse to do "war work," and she and other teachers at Washington School collected money for the American Red Cross. She commented on Liberty Loan Institutes held at Purdue and Thrift Stamps. Liberty Bonds or Loans were introduced as a means of financing the war. The purchase of Liberty Bonds became a symbol of patriotism, and the bonds were many Americans' first introduction to the idea of financial securities. However, the first issue of these bonds did not sell well, which embarrassed the Treasury Department. In response, when they issued their second offering in late 1917, they launched an aggressive public awareness campaign using famous artists to make posters and movie stars to host rallies. Al Jolson, Mary Pickford, Douglas Fairbanks, and Charlie Chaplin were among the celebrities who made public appearances to promote Liberty Bonds.

An elite group of Army pilots was assigned to the Liberty Bond campaign. The pilots crisscrossed the county in their Curtis J4 "Jenny" training aircraft. Lella and Kate's nephew, Paul, flew a Jenny. The family called the campaign "Bond Selling Tours." When the pilots arrived over a town, they performed acrobatic stunts, then landed in a nearby pasture or on a road. Most people had never seen an airplane, let alone had a chance to ride in one, so by the time the pilots shut down their engines, the townspeople would have gathered to see the spectacle. Each pilot then stood in the rear cockpit of his craft and announced that every person who purchased a Liberty Bond would receive a ride in one of the airplanes. The program raised a substantial amount of money. Years later, Paul's daughter, Mary Louise Riley Van Camp Pickering, said, "I remember Daddy talking of the fun of 'hedgehopping' on Bond Selling Tours." After the war, entrepreneurial flyers called Barnstormers purchased war surplus Jenny planes and flew across the country selling airplane rides. During the war, Kate noticed the skies over Tippecanoe County: "September 22: Papa's birthday today. Instead of flowers [for his grave], I get yarn for socks for some soldiers. Lots of airplanes around now."

Thrift Stamps were another way of financing the war while instilling traditional values. They were issued by the Treasury Department to encourage thrift and support of the effort among those Americans who could not afford even the smallest Liberty Bond. Thrift Stamps cost twenty-five cents each, and when sixteen were collected, they could be exchanged for War Savings Stamps or Certificates, which bore interest of 4% and were tax free. May 6, 1918 was declared "National Thrift Stamp Day" with special drives throughout the country. For the day, merchants throughout the United States adopted the slogan, "Take your change in Thrift Stamps." Often, Thrift Stamps were targeted to immigrants and schoolchildren. As a teacher, Kate was involved. She writes:

> April 11: We are busy working for Thrift Stamps in our room at school. Wonderful how they like it.
>
> August 19: My birthday today. Mack gave me Thrift Stamps and lots of love.
>
> September 28: Fourth Liberty Loan today. We have $350. Am glad we can do it. Seems so little.

On April 29, Kate noted that five hundred soldiers arrived that day to "Camp Purdue." When the selective service legislation drafted young men, colleges and universities lost their enrollment and feared they were doomed. At the opening of the school year of 1917-1918, there was a 25% reduction in students and faculty. Purdue introduced the Students' Army Training Corps (SATC) and made an appeal to thousands of male students across the country. Eleven hundred Purdue students registered for the SATC. Purdue University's Dean Stanley Coulter was superintendent of the Purdue SATC.

Under the terms of its contract with the War Department, the University agreed to house, feed, and train fifteen hundred men from October 1, 1918, to June 30, 1919. The government pledged to pay one dollar per man per day for room and board and twelve cents for tuition. Five buildings were constructed along with sheds to house equipment and Army trucks. A recreational building was also constructed that housed the Knights of Columbus, the Jewish Welfare Society, and the YMCA. In her journals, Kate mentioned stopping to see the camp buildings on an October Sunday. These were all temporary structures that were salvaged after their term of use. Special courses were organized on campus in wireless telegraphy, bayonet practice, semaphore flag signaling, Army regulations, the care of gas motors in aviation, first aid, and more.

Dean of Women Carolyn Shoemaker created a "Hostess House" for soldiers at the Phi Delta Theta fraternity. Wives, mothers, and friends of the soldiers were welcomed overnight there until they found rooms elsewhere. Dances were held at the Hostess House as well. As Kate records on July 14, "We went to the Hostess House this morning. Only the Military police in."

❦

Months before the war ended, the country was hit with another kind of battle—the most serious flu epidemic of the century. Home demonstration agents took the lead to aid the county health departments during the 1918 influenza emergency. In many instances, they served as nurses and dieticians. Lella was now in charge of a health campaign that included training women in the care of the sick and better nutrition for children. Most public meetings were banned to stop the transmission of the flu virus. Kate's school was closed for a month. She writes:

> October 5: See order in the paper no school next week. Influenza and pneumonia.

> November 4: School opened again today. The war looks very encouraging. Don't think the Kaiser will hold out much longer. Over none too soon.

Kate was referring to Kaiser Wilhelm II, the last German emperor and king of Prussia, who abdicated his throne and went into exile in the Netherlands at the end of the World War I.

> November 11: World Wide War ends today. Paul home. Armistice signed this morning. No school. Celebrate all day.

> November 12: Back to school today. The Nation wild with joy. Oh, how glad we all are. The war ends the eleventh month, the eleventh day, the eleventh hour. I Kings 11-11.

> > Therefore the Lord said to Solomon,
> > "Since this has been your mind and
> > you have not kept my covenant and

> my statues which I have commanded you,
> I will surely tear the Kingdom from you
> and will give it to your servant . . ."

1 Kings 11:11
Revised Standard Version Bible

Lella and Kate's nephew, Paul, was home on leave just prior to being shipped overseas when the Armistice was signed on November 11. He would not have to go to Europe. He returned to Mitchell Field, Long Island, New York, where he had been previously stationed and was discharged from the service in December 1918. He arrived home very sick with the flu that had taken so many lives that year. His wife, Ruth, and mother, Mamie, nursed him back to health. The day Paul returned, Ruth and Mamie struggled to remove Paul's boots, which came to the knees. He was too weak to help them.

By the end of 1918, things were looking up in America with the end of both the influenza outbreak and the war. The Gaddis sisters and Mary Matthews had spent the war years working hard to win the effort on the home front. Lella and Kate's grandmother died at age 102 on a snowy day in February. The women traveled to the funeral in Rossville by bobsled. Also that month, their friend and boarder Anna Roberta McNeill ("Mack") moved to South Dakota to live near her beau, Dave Whitton. She received a diamond engagement ring that Christmas. Kate missed her friend, and she said Mack, whom she described as "lovesick," left "without a tear or sigh." In March of 1919, Kate wrote Mack an eighteen-page letter, and she commented in her diary, "Dave seems housebroke." Mack married and eventually had two sons. Through the years, she kept in contact with Kate by letter.

In addition, in 1918, the sister's good friend and Lella's superior George Christie was named United States Assistant Secretary of Agriculture. Kate writes on April 9, "Mr. Christie to have a position in Washington. Good-bye G. I."

Roaring Women

In Purdue's 1919 *Debris* yearbook, a coed wrote a poem lamenting the poor conditions in which she and her fellow female students endured to attend classes in Ladies Hall, then used solely as an instructional facility and not a residence hall:

The Coed's Plea

You have talked of cows and horses,
     You've talked of pigs and sheep,
You've talked of your new horse barn,
     In which horses you will keep.

But when you're talking of all this,
     You never stop to say,
"We wonder if our fair coeds
     Would like a place to stay."

And all this time I madly rushed
     On toward Ladies' Hall;
I put my face inside the door
     Just where the plaster falls.

I went into the kitchen lab,
    Where I would make some bread,
And when I had the sponge all set,
    Some plaster struck my head.

By this time it was getting dark,
    We could not see to bake.
We struck just twenty matches, then
    Found lights to be a fake.

And now, Purdue, you wonder why
    We're sour and cross today.
It's all because we coeds few
    Are treated in this way.

                    —Excerpted from 1919 *Debris*, author unknown

Ladies Hall, also known at one time as Art Hall, was built in 1872 and was the first permanent building north of State Street on the Purdue University campus. When Purdue opened in 1874, it housed the college dining room, living quarters for new faculty and their families, and the office for Purdue's first president, Abraham C. Shortridge. For most of its existence, it was a women's residence hall and classroom facility. Ladies Hall was torn down in 1927.
Courtesy of Purdue University Libraries, Archives and Special Collections.

In addition, Dean of Women Carolyn Shoemaker wrote an essay lobbying for the "promise of a Woman's Building." She said, "$150,000 is no small item when we come to consider what its expenditure may mean." She explained that the enrollment of girls had doubled in the previous few years, and there were 247 young women at Purdue that year. She enumerated the activities in which the girls participated, including the YWCA, sororities, honor societies, Purdue Girls' Glee Club, and the Girls' Ukulele Club. She also commended women's "war work in all its phases" and their support of the legislation regulating the hours and working conditions of women in industry. She ended her piece on a high note: "This, in fine, is the Purdue spirit. Progressive? Yes. And we have accomplished it all with no place that is peculiarly our own. But with a Woman's Building with headquarters for our various activities,—well, just watch us and see!" Shoemaker was referring to the new Home Economics Building that would be constructed under Mary Matthews's leadership in 1922 at the corner of West State and University Streets, today known as Matthews Hall.

Mary's accomplishments for the School of Home Economics and women at Purdue were made possible in part by her perceptive understanding that she needed connections with those in power. One of those important figures was Dean Andrey Abraham Potter, known as A. A. Potter. Potter was a nationally known figure in engineering and scientific education who was born in Russia. After reading the autobiography of Benjamin Franklin, Potter's dream as a young boy was to come to the United States. He accomplished that goal when he was fifteen. He entered the Massachusetts Institute of Technology (MIT) at age seventeen, earning a degree in mechanical engineering. One of his instructors was Ellen Swallow Richards, the "original home economics superwoman." She was an international expert in water quality and was the first woman instructor at MIT, teaching there until her death. In the early 1900s, she organized the Lake Placid Conferences that elevated home economics to a legitimate profession. She opened doors for women in science and walked ground no woman had touched before. Potter often told stories of what it was like as a student to be entertained in the Richards's household.

Potter worked for General Electric Company in New York before becoming an assistant professor of mechanical engineering in the Kansas State Agricultural College where he established one of the first curricula in agricultural engineering. In 1906, he became a U.S. citizen and married Eva Burtner, a domestic science graduate of Kansas State Agricultural College. Later he was named dean of engineering and director of the Engineering Experiment Station at Kansas State. In 1920, Potter joined Purdue University as dean of the School of Engineering. Under his leadership, engineering at Purdue expanded and became one of the largest and most respected programs in the country. Potter was affectionately referred to as "The Dean of Deans" because of the important role he played in engineering education in America during the twentieth century.

Potter had an affinity for home economics because of his admiration and friendship with Ellen Swallow Richards and the fact that his wife held a degree in domestic science. During a talk to a home economics audience after his retirement, he shared some of his memories of Ellen Richards, the visionary leader who could see how all things worked together: "To those who knew Ellen Richards, and worked with her, she is remembered as the vivacious and kindly leader, inspiring teacher, counselor, practical scientist, devoted friend and one who was giving of herself to inspire happier lives for others. She also had time for abundant hospitality in her home and demonstrated that a woman can contribute to improvement of the environment in which people live and work."

It is no wonder that Potter took a liking to Mary Matthews, who was made dean of Purdue's School of Home Economics six years after his arrival. In many ways, Mary emulated the traits of Ellen Richards. Often, Potter said, "Miss Matthews was a lady, a perfect lady." Vianna Dezinang Bramblett, an early staff member, said, "Sometimes I felt she ought to 'blow up' or fight more. She would prepare carefully worked out justifications as to why certain of her staff should be advanced in rank or increased in salary, then go to a meeting with the other administrators (all men) and the men would voter her down! That did hurt Miss Matthews keenly; but she kept right on trying and remaining a LADY!"

The "lady" did win some major battles. She was responsible for the first married woman allowed to remain working at Purdue. She established a new Home Economics Building and several groundbreaking areas. With Potter as a mentor, Mary made headway for home economics. In 2010, Dean Emeritus Eva Goble said of Mary:

I have a lot of respect for what she got done. In the first place, she kept her lines open with Dean Potter, Dean Potter's wife, and President Elliott. The staff had a lot of respect for her opinion. She established new departments, and she could see they were needed. We didn't have a department of consumer and family life. We didn't have a nursery school. We didn't have anything but the lunch program. She got these things established, and she protected the money so she could do it. Establishing the different departments as they were needed and finding staff for them—that was a big job because there weren't many people trained for it. I think she deserves a lot of credit.

Kate Gaddis writes of Potter in her diary on December 8, 1922: "Teachers Council Dinner. Dean Potter talked on Character Building. He is alive to his subject."

Mary was very conscious of her role as a leader in the home economics profession, and she wanted that image to be a good one. Vianna Dezinang Bramblett said, "She was a pioneer in home economics, she believed in it 100%. She believed it was a profession anyone could be proud to be associated with, and there were great opportunities in the profession for the betterment of home, family, and for happier living for both women and men."

Another factor that aided Mary in her home economic pursuits was her mother's historic position that had been granted in 1921. That year the Indiana General Assembly passed a bill requiring that more alumni be appointed to the Purdue University Board of Trustees. The new law also required the governor to select at least one woman among the six appointments. The women's suffrage movement had put pressure on all public institutions to appoint qualified women when board positions became available. Indiana Governor Warren T. McCray selected Virginia Meredith, age seventy-two, as the first female member of the Purdue University Board of Trustees. Virginia attended her first board meeting in July in Eliza Fowler Hall, a building that stood where today's Stewart Center is located. She knew many of her male colleagues including David E. Ross, one of the principal benefactors of, among other Purdue landmarks, Ross-Ade Stadium. Virginia's first board meeting proved momentous for several reasons. One particular agenda item was sweet destiny for Virginia. At her initial meeting as

Purdue's first woman trustee, she voted with the board to authorize the construction of the Home Economics Building—the structure that would one day be named after her daughter.

President Winthrop E. Stone and his wife, Margaret, on one of their many mountain climbing expeditions before his startling death and her heroic survival. Courtesy of Purdue University Libraries, Archives and Special Collections.

Purdue President Winthrop Stone was an avid mountain climber. In the spring of 1920, Kate Gaddis went to a lecture "to hear Dr. Stone tell of his mountain climbing." At the July 21, 1921, board meeting, he asked for permission to take a vacation that month. He and his wife, Margaret, wanted to travel to Canada to be the first to climb to the summit of Eon Mountain in the Canadian Rockies. The trustees chuckled about Stone's request, yet granted him the time off. Little did they know, it would be their last and Virginia's only meeting with Stone.

Stone's final gesture before leaving West Lafayette for his mountain climbing expedition was to pick a basket of roses from his garden at his white-frame home on Grant Street. He delivered the roses to Blanche Miller, a staff member of the Purdue library. Miller was the friend and unofficial advisor to Purdue Presidents Smart, Stone, Elliott, and Hovde. (She held the longest tenure of any Purdue staff member from the 1890s to the 1950s.) Stone's gift of roses to Blanche was one of the kind and thoughtful acts his colleagues and friends often remembered about him.

The peak of Eon Mountain rises nearly eleven thousand feet above sea level. Stone would be the first person credited with climbing the peak, and Margaret would be credited with her own amazing feat. In the evening of July 17, the couple had almost reached the summit. Stone left his wife on a ledge that was forty feet below the actual peak and continued climbing to explore the area. Margaret shouted at him, asking if he was near the top, and he replied, "I see nothing higher." Suddenly, the rocks gave way, and he fell one thousand feet to his death. Conrad Kain, part of the search party for the Stones, explained the scenario, "Without any warning, a large slab of rock tumbled off from above, passing over Mrs. Stone, and was closely followed by Dr. Stone, who spoke no word but held his ice-axe firmly in his right hand. Horror stricken at the sight, Mrs. Stone braced herself to take the jerk of the rope, not realizing that [her husband] had taken it off to explore beyond its length."

The accident occurred at about 6:00 p.m., and Margaret spent the night, in shock, close to the summit. Her water, food, sweater, and other provisions were all in her husband's pack. The following day, Margaret looked for her husband unsuccessfully, and then descended to the lower cliffs. She spent seven days without food or significant water until rescuers were able to reach her. Then she was carried for four and a half hours on the back of one of her rescuers to a safe area. A raft was built to carry Margaret along Marvel Lake. It was August 10 when she had recovered to the point where she could reach Bow Valley. Margaret sent a telegram to her late husband's secretary, Helen Hand, informing her of the president's death. An Associated Press release had been the only other word received on campus until Margaret sent the personal note about the tragedy. Stone was fifty-nine at the time of his death.

The rescue party found Stone's body jammed between the sides of a seventeen-foot-deep crevice. Before taking his body down, the team climbed to Eon's summit, built a rock cairn, and crowned it with Stone's ice axe. They left a small metal box with a note inside that said in part: "This monument was built . . . in tribute to their comrade of the mountains, Dr. Winthrop E. Stone, President of Purdue University, Lafayette, Indiana, U.S.A."

Jon Whyte, a Canadian who embraced "mountain writing," wrote a poem about the tragedy. It begins:

> **The Agony of Mrs. Stone**
> A statement isolated
> between a question it poses
> a question unanswered-
> how she endured seven days
> on the mountain
> Her husband fell
> from the summit of Eon
> into death's isolation
> "I can see nothing higher"
> he had shouted
> from the mountain's height

Kate notes in her 1921 diary:

> July 26: See by the Indianapolis News that Dr. Stone and Mrs. Stone are lost in the mountains.
>
> July 27: They found Dr. Stone dead and Mrs. Stone badly hurt. Had been in a crevice for 10 days.

A few days later, Lella and Kate took a train to Chicago, then boarded the Manitou Steamer Ship to sail to Charlevoix, Michigan, where they stayed on Pine Lake, renamed Lake Charlevoix in 1926. They were guests of Professor of Agriculture William Latta, then age seventy-one, and his wife, Alta, who owned a cottage there at Eveline Orchards. Eveline Orchards was three hundred acres of apple, cherry, and plum trees developed and sold by Levi R. Taft, head of the Horticulture Department at Michigan Agricultural College. He sold land along the Lake Charlevoix shoreline as a resort area, and the funds supported the orchard. Taft and Latta used the orchard to run experiments on fruit trees. Latta was one of the first buyers, purchasing a lot for $50 in 1910. The following year, he built his summer cottage "BER-OPAMA," which was a name he created using the first two letters of his children's names. The Latta family spent every summer at BER-OPAMA. In 1921, Lella and Kate were invited for a visit. While there, they helped sew the wedding dress for Latta's daughter, Pauline, who would be married that year. Of course, Kate packed her diary and recorded her time amid the woods, cool air, and lapping water, yet she was never far from thoughts of Purdue: "August 9: Took a long ride in a small steamer around the lake. We hear that they found Dr. Stone's body."

Months after Virginia became a trustee, she began discussions about renovation of Ladies Hall, which was forty-seven years old and exhibited unsafe conditions for women students. The women needed a residence hall. During the early 1920s, the hundreds of female students at Purdue struggled to obtain housing. Some lived in sororities, others resided at home with their parents, and some were lucky enough to live in cooperative houses that Purdue rented from local residents. (Some girls were boarders of Lella and Kate Gaddis.) Embarrassingly, other young Purdue women found room and board by working as cooks, maids, and servants in the community. This was not acceptable to Virginia. She believed Purdue coeds deserved their own dormitory.

Perhaps Virginia was also thinking of an incident that occurred in 1920. In a videotaped interview from 1995, Vern Freeman, retired associate dean of the School of Agriculture, shared an experience when he was "Mary Matthews's Armed Deputy." On the tape, Vern held a microphone as he settled into his story. Vern said:

> The Purdue campus at that time was an armed camp. . . . This was just in the aftermath of WWI. I was wearing an Army uniform. As an armed camp with very few ladies around, the men were very protective. . . . I was going over to North Marsteller Street to catch up with a young lady . . . , a member of Alpha Xi Delta. There were prowlers around this house . . . with probably twenty-five girls, and they reported to Mary Matthews about this [the prowlers]. . . . This young lady that I was meeting mentioned my name as being a hunter and a good man with a gun, which was true. Mary Matthews contacted me, and gave me her .32 caliber Smith and Wesson revolver, loaded, and she said, "Vern, I want you to protect those girls over there at this house on Marsteller."

During the spring of 1920, Vern spent every evening patrolling the Marsteller house dressed in his Army uniform and armed with Mary's Smith and Wesson. Occasionally, the girls would step outside and spend time with Vern who saw no prowlers during his "duty." He continued his story with a playful grin: "Now, I imagine my presence was a very great safety factor for these young ladies. The sequel to this story is that I was able to complete my task without ever firing a single shot."

The *prequel* to the story was Mary owned a gun, and she was not afraid to put it to good use.

Virginia Meredith formed a committee to determine the future of Ladies Hall. Now that the new Home Economics Building was available for classes, the committee recommended to the Purdue University Board of Trustees that Ladies Hall be renovated and used as a temporary dormitory until an adequate women's dormitory could be erected. They listed the many repairs necessary. Among other antiquated characteristics, the building still had gaslights that needed to be converted to electric. The board reviewed bids for the proposed list of renovations and found them to exceed the price they wanted to spend. In the end, they put just enough money into the project to keep the building useful, and Ladies Hall housed fewer than fifty women.

Five years later, the cost for more repairs again exceeded what the board was willing to spend, and the building was torn down that summer. One of the last of Purdue's five original buildings was gone. Virginia believed that the demise of Ladies Hall would speed up the building of a women's dormitory. After all, fifty women had been displaced. She pointed out that most land-grant colleges in the Midwest already had modern residence halls for coeds.

Kate commented on the building's demise in her 1927 journal. She writes, "They are tearing down Ladies Hall at Purdue and building a 6-foot tunnel. Some torn up."

As Ladies Hall came tumbling down, Purdue administrators again leased rooms for women students in local homes. The Vater house at 415 West State Street in West Lafayette was rented for $1,000 a year. The women paid rent, and the University broke even on the deal. The building was referred to as the housing annex for women students. Another home was the George Dexter house at 116 Marsteller Street where today's Marsteller Parking Garage is located. This house was also the office and home of Dean of Women Carolyn Shoemaker. Knowing that renting homes was a temporary fix to the women's housing shortage, then President Edward Elliott and the board assigned Virginia to chair another committee to investigate women's residence halls offered at other universities. This committee was comprised of a Purdue women's who's who of the time. Members were Dean Carolyn Shoemaker, Dean Mary Matthews, Lella Gaddis, and Professor Gertrude Bilhuber, head of the Department of Physical Education for Women. Purdue Controller Robert B. Stewart was the only man on the committee. President Elliott and David Ross, president of the board, were *ex officio* members.

Virginia's committee met several times in the fall of 1927, and then she learned that well-known donors wanted to support the building of a women's residence hall. Frank M. and Jessie Levering Cary had previously given $50,000 for the building of a men's dormitory in memory of their late son, Franklin Levering Cary, who had been preparing to enter Purdue when he died at the age of eighteen. Levering Cary Memorial Hall, today named Cary East as part of Cary Quadrangle, was made possible with the Cary's donation combined with money Purdue borrowed. Then in 1928, Frank Cary offered another $60,000 to build a residence hall for women to be named in memory of his wife, who had just passed away. Virginia was most appreciative and thanked Cary in a heartfelt resolution read to the board. Frank Cary and the trustees signed a contract, and the board assured Cary that they would borrow sufficient money to complete the women's residence hall. With the go-ahead for the project, Virginia and the other trustees decided they would no longer lease the home on Marsteller Street. As a result, Dean Carolyn Shoemaker lost her office and was given temporary quarters in the Engineering Administration Building.

During the dedication of the new Women's Residence Hall (now Duhme Hall) in 1934, Mary Rose Harlan and Edith Jones presented a time capsule to place in the cornerstone. It included a memorial to Dean Carolyn Shoemaker who had passed away unexpectedly the previous year. Standing are Virginia C. Meredith, David E. Ross, President Edward Elliott, Dean of Women Dorothy Stratton, architect Walter Scholer, Indiana Federation of Clubs representative Mrs. Frank Sheehan, alumnae representative Mrs. R.D. Canan, and Director of Women's Residence Hall Helen Schleman. Courtesy of Purdue University Libraries, Archives and Special Collections.

The plan was that the women's dormitory would be built north of State Street on property referred to as "Russell land," on Russell Street today. Purdue expected to acquire this land from owner Phillip Russell. Years before Russell's parents had donated land to John Purdue for his construction of Purdue University, but the apple fell far from the tree with this offspring. Phillip was not as generous as his parents. The women's residence hall project faced barrier after barrier due to suits and countersuits as Purdue tried to gain control of the Russell property by condemnation through eminent domain. The issue inched its way through the legal system and eventually ended up before the Indiana Supreme Court. By 1930, Phillip Russell filed yet another legal action against Purdue University, and this bad news was the final straw for Frank Cary. The deal was off. He eventually found another setting to memorialize his late wife. He built the Jessie Levering Cary Home for Children on South 18th Street in Lafayette, and it is still in operation today.

Though Frank Cary would not donate funds to build a women's dormitory, he agreed to give his $60,000 toward building another men's dormitory near the first Cary Hall. Purdue did not want to lose the funding, so the board, including Virginia, agreed that the donation would go to another men's dorm. By this time, Virginia must have felt the cards were stacked against her. In retrospect, it looks as if the male-dominated administration was playing with a "marked deck" and not placing a high priority on bringing women students to Purdue. Virginia had spent nine years working for better housing for women with nothing to show for her efforts, and Purdue's enrollment of women was in jeopardy. Why would women choose to attend Purdue if there was not adequate and safe housing? It appears excuses were made. Bids came in "too high," the designated land was in a legal battle, and the men in administration wondered how many women would actually be able to afford and want to stay in the new dormitory.

Yet the Russell land was still the property slated for a new women's dorm. Finally, in 1934, legal proceedings ended with an Indiana Supreme Court decision transferring title on 32.45 acres of Russell's property to Purdue University for $32,002, which included land for the women's dorm and an intramural field. With funds from the Depression-era Public Works Administration (PWA) and a bank loan, the University fast-tracked the building of the new dormitory, officially named the Women's Residence Hall. Today it is called Duhme and is one of five buildings forming Windsor Halls. The new Women's Residence Hall was dedicated as part of homecoming events on October 20, 1934, with Virginia, then eighty-five, presiding. The event included a cornerstone ceremony with a time capsule. Some of the contents of the box placed in the cornerstone were brochures on the activities and curriculum for women, copies of the Purdue *Exponent* newspaper, a Bible, and a memorial to Dean Carolyn Shoemaker. Shoemaker had died unexpectedly the previous year from nephritis, caused by inflammation of the kidney. The first Dean of Women did not live to see the realization of her Purdue dream she shared with Virginia. Kate writes in her diary, "Dean Shoemaker found unconscious in her apartment at 5 p.m. She died at 10:30 at St. Elizabeth. A good friend of the girls."

At the time, Lella and Kate lived at 221 North Russell Street. The address of the new Women's Residence hall was 205 North Russell Street. Kate may have feared the tall, brick Tudor style residence hall would shade their property or perhaps trees were taken out, and more sunlight was a plus to the women's home. She writes on September 9: "The new girls' dorm done, and we have lots of light in the back."

Kate makes no mention of she or Lella attending the dedication of the Women's Residence Hall built a few doors away from their home. Perhaps they saw it as a Virginia Meredith and Mary Matthews function, and the Gaddis sisters were more akin to the goings on in the School of Agriculture. The following year, on April 5, Kate writes of the new dormitory, "Lella was over at the Residence hall for dinner last night. I have never been over yet."

The Women's Residence Hall was built to accommodate 119 women, and 112 applications were received when it opened in 1934. The next year, there were 189 applications for housing there. Amelia Earhart would stay at the Women's Residence Hall after President Edward Elliott appointed her a visiting faculty member with the titles of consultant on women's careers and advisor in aeronautics. In 1932, Earhart was the first woman to fly the Atlantic solo and the only person to fly it twice. Five days before the new Women's Residence Hall was dedicated, President Elliott hosted Earhart on a campus visit in hopes of wooing her to develop a relationship with Purdue. Purdue Controller R. B. Stewart once summed up Earhart's Purdue job as

"motivating the girls to do something more than take home economics courses and work on the (men-women) ratio on the campus." During her first visit to Purdue, Earhart spoke to the faculty and women
students on "Opportunities for Women in Aviation." Lella and Kate
were in the audience, and Kate writes of it in her diary: "October 16:
The University Club party. Amelia Earhart there. Wear my new blue
lace dress."

It took Virginia Meredith thirteen years to achieve the creation of
a women's dormitory at Purdue University. She dedicated the building "to the happy and useful living of Purdue women students." President Elliott had a new women's dormitory to show off to Amelia
Earhart. In large part, it was Virginia's vision that made it possible.

It would be forty-three years later when a women's residence hall
would be named after the woman who persevered for all Purdue females. At the Purdue University Board of Trustees meeting on June 5,
1965, then President Hovde presented a proposal for "Naming of
University Residence Facilities" as a solution to a long-term problem.
He explained that it was "time to replace letter names for the various
halls, particularly the 'H' halls." That day, Men's Residences H-1
through H-5 were named after five great Purdue men: Richard Owen,
Newton Booth Tarkington, Harvey W. Wiley, John T. McCutcheon,
and Benjamin Harrison. Two women's residences were christened after distinguished Purdue women. Women's Residence H-8 was named
Amelia Earhart Hall, and Women's Residence Hall X (the building is
shaped like an "X") was named Virginia C. Meredith Hall. Mary Matthews was eighty-three years old when she saw a women's residence
hall named in honor of her mother.

Vote of Confidence

On August 18, 1920, American women received the right to vote. The ratification of the 19th Amendment to the United States Constitution was a triumph after decades of long and difficult struggles by thousands of women. Beginning in the mid-nineteenth century, suffragists lectured, wrote, marched, lobbied, and practiced civil disobedience to achieve what many Americans considered a radical change in the Constitution. Few of the women who rallied for the vote in the early years lived to see final victory in 1920. The first time they voted and had a say in their country's government, Mary Matthews was thirty-eight, Virginia Meredith was seventy-two, Lella Gaddis was forty-three, and Kate Gaddis was fifty-two. In her diary, Kate takes readers into the world of 1920 and the first Election Day when American women could mark a ballot:

> February 21: Went to the Citizen's Meeting to learn to vote and found out I am a Republican.

> November 2: Came home from school and cast my first vote.

> November 3: Such a landslide for the Republicans was never heard of.

Warren G. Harding was elected in the 1920 election, and Kate records her own spin on Harding's win: "March 4, 1921: A new president. Warren G. Harding. Poor Woodrow Wilson is a wreck."

In *Taking the University to the People: Seventy-Five Years of Cooperative Extension* by Wayne D. Rasmussen, he states, "The women who came into extension work early and made it a lifetime career had rural backgrounds, a good basic education, good communication skills and a sense of mission" (p. 87). To perfection, those words describe Lella Gaddis, first state leader of home demonstration. Lella grew up on a farm in Rossville, Indiana; she had a Purdue education; she was not afraid to speak her mind and tell people how things should be done; and most importantly, she exuded an inner fire of purpose to better the lives of rural women. After World War I, many of the emergency home demonstration agents were discharged. In 1920, Lella had only two agents in Indiana—one in Hendricks County and another in Vanderburgh County. With her forces depleted within the counties, she and her agents trained farm women in leadership techniques and equipped them with skills that enabled them to teach others in their Home Economics Clubs. Actually, the shortage of agents helped rural women even more by giving them opportunities in management-like roles and public speaking—positions that were very foreign territory for farm women of the time. In DeKalb County, Lella helped organize the Franklin Township Club. Many of the women walked miles to this meeting, as the horses were busy performing farm work and could not be used for transportation.

Each club chose two women who were trained by a Purdue specialist about the information they would demonstrate to their clubs and on their presentation techniques. This guidance gave women the experience and confidence to become leaders in their community in many areas, not just home economics.

A popular demonstration at that time was the "Dress Form Project." With the homemade dress form, a woman made an economical, exact duplicate of her figure by using gummed paper, similar to masking tape. When sewing for herself, a woman could fit her garment on the dress form and tailor it to her exact proportions. The making of a dress form took patience and, often times, a sense of humor. The

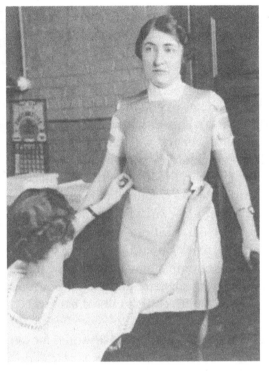

A *popular early home demonstration was the "Dress Form Project." Gummed paper was dipped in water and wrapped around the torso. When dried, it often constricted breathing and some women fainted. The dried paper was cut from the body and used as a form to fit garments when sewing.* Courtesy of Purdue University Libraries, Archives and Special Collections.

woman for whom the dress form was being created had to stand perfectly still and erect, so her helpers, about four per person, tried to work quickly. First, the woman put on a tight-fitting cloth garment over her underwear. Then strips of gummed paper were dipped into water and wrapped snugly around her entire body from neck to below the hips. She would be covered with as much as three thicknesses of tape, which was uncomfortable and wet. Once the form dried and was stiff, it was so tight the chest could not expand, and many women fainted.

Going to Club by Eleanor Arnold is the fifth in a series of books called *Memories of Hoosier Homemakers.* Arnold compiled the book in celebration of the 75th anniversary of the founding of the Indiana Extension Homemakers Association in 1988. She and her volunteers interviewed nearly three hundred Indiana homemakers in 1980 for an oral history project that provided the content for the book. *Going to Club* contains quotes from Indiana women about what Home Economics Clubs meant to them. Hazel Norden, age seventy-six in 1980, said, "The Extension club has just been the answer for everything for me." Pat Ritchey, 47 at that time, echoed Norden's experience: "It's a way of getting a college education without going to college."

Several women remembered making dress forms in their Home Economics Clubs. Marie Unfried, age seventy-one, of Vanderburgh County said, "Well, this lady, we got a good start on her and she started to faint on us, and we didn't know what to do. We couldn't lay her down, we couldn't sit her down and we didn't know whether to cut her out of it and ruin it—we didn't know really what to do. . . . A group got around her and we was [sic] holding her in our arms, and another group was there fanning her and washing her face and trying to bring her to. We worked with her until we did get her out of it [the faint], and we asked her if she wanted to continue with the dress form, and she said yes. So we stood her back up and continued with her dress form. But the clinch was that evening when we all went home. We didn't use cars much then; we were all there in the neighborhood. And to see them all walking down the street with these dress forms in their arms!"

Once the form dried and hardened, it was cut in half and removed. The two parts were taped back together and the form was placed on a stand. Dean Emeritus of the School of Home Economics Eva Goble, age one hundred in 2010, remembered teaching women how to make dress forms: "I made one for the home agent once, and when I cut it off, I didn't know she'd kept her girdle on. I cut her girdle!"

Kate wrote a couple of lines about this project and mentioned Mrs. Skinner, the wife of Dean of Agriculture John H. Skinner.

> December 3, 1920: Finish paying for my Victrola today. We do enjoy it so much. Girls made my dress form last night.
>
> April 22, 1921: Lella at the Skinners to make Mrs. S. a dress form.

Home demonstration agents also brought the "Mattress Project" to farm families who had never had mattresses before. Prior to learning how to make their own, they slept on blankets on the floor. The agents taught the women how to sew large cloth mattress cases and fill them with bales of cotton. Both men and women worked on the mattresses because it took a couple of people to handle their unwieldy size.

Chickens and milk cows were often the farm wife's responsibility. Early extension lessons taught advantages of different breeds of chickens, how to make cottage and hoop cheeses, and how to pick "good pullets" to put in the laying house for the winter. Hoop cheese is a traditional "farmer's cheese" made by draining the whey from a cottage cheese then placing the curd into a round mold (the hoop) and pressing it out. Chickens more than a year old are hens, and younger females are pullets. Farm women took their eggs to grocery stores and sold them to make money for groceries. One of the early demonstration topics was "taking care of eggs."

A "good white wash" was the mark of a fine homemaker back then, so lessons on laundry were welcomed. Women learned the proper techniques to hang laundry on a clothesline to reduce wrinkles and wear and tear on garments and linens. Extension demonstrations also included better ways to make homemade soap. Of course, cooking instructions were popular, especially those that taught new ways to use the limited variety of foods available. Laborsaving methods of preparing food helped women who had to work from morning to night to accomplish all of their tasks. Florence LaGrange, 79, of Perry County said, "I did my canning at night. I'd have my kerosene lamp setting up on the range top. It was all I had. I don't know how many flies we canned, because we couldn't see."

Another woman's story tells of her "drive" to learn new techniques. Vernell Saltzman, 83, of Posey County remembered, "They came down from Purdue to teach us how to cold pack and prepare our food and save it. I drove a horse and buggy halfway, and I met up with Carlene Cowan Ramsey. She had a car. I could drive a car straight forward, but I could not back one, so I picked her up . . . and we worked all day canning. When we got ready to go home, Carlene couldn't drive the car down straight, but she could back it, so she backed it up, and I drove the car home and got my horse and buggy."

The demonstration was the central feature of the extension lesson, as exemplified by an unknown author in a poem entitled "The Demonstration Way":

I'd rather see a lesson
Than hear one any day.
I'd rather you would walk with me
Than merely show the way.

The eye's a better teacher
And more willing than the ear.
And counsel is confusing;
But example's always clear.

The best of all the teachers
Are those who live their creeds,
For to see good put in action
Is what everybody needs.

I can soon learn to do it
If you let me see it done.
I can watch your hands in action,
But your tongue too fast may run.

And the counsel you are giving
May be very fine and true,
But I'd rather get my lesson
By observing what you do.

Food was prepared before their eyes and later eaten. Basket weaving and other craft classes included supplies for each participant to make her own creation as she watched the leader. A sewing lesson would involve the leader bringing a portable sewing machine or borrowing the hostess's and actually sewing before the club, demonstrating how to make a buttonhole or patch overalls. Children's clothes were made from printed flour or feed sacks. Many of the feed companies put feed in flowered bags that made pretty dresses for little girls. Extension agents gave lessons on how to make hats and gloves, both fashion staples of the day. The gloves were sewn out of a chamois made for washing windows. Women dyed fabric, cut it into strips, and made hooked rugs.

Health lessons included a series on nursing with a nurse demonstrating in front of the club how to give a patient a bath. Nurses attended meetings and weighed children to see if they were gaining and healthy. Programs included baby care and child rearing. This was before people took their babies to physicians for wellness checkups. There were lessons on polio, rheumatic fever, mental health, and food poisoning.

Meetings often lasted all day. Club members might come at 10:00 a.m. for the first part of a lesson, break for a carry-in lunch, and then continue the lesson or have a business meeting in the afternoon. Children tagged along and played under the quilting frame, in the yard, or in a spare room. Often the children outnumbered the women.

In *Going to Club*, Lillian Gookins, age seventy-six, of Jennings County described the beginning of Home Economics Clubs and the "lady from Purdue." She said:

> In 1923, Purdue started a new project. They were going to send letters out to different counties, and they would bring lessons. And women could come in and get the lesson. Then they wanted them to go back home and get their neighbors and friends in and teach them the lessons they had learned from the lady from Purdue. I remember when Lella Gaddis came down. She was one of the first instructors. . . . mostly at the time it was sewing. . . . Then after we had our four lessons, they asked us to get a group in and organize. So that's when we organized into Home Economics Clubs.

Lora Herrick, eighty-nine, from Cass County also had memories of Lella. Lora said, "She was very likeable. She got around to see everybody. She was very capable in getting people to do things. She had to be capable to hold down a job as big as that was and to keep it going. She came to our county meetings. I don't know how she got around like she did, but she had very good health."

One of the comments in *Going to Club* sums up the essence of the land-grant university and tells of the effect Purdue had on rural woman in the first half of the twentieth century. Lillian Gookins said, "Back in the beginning, most of the people at that time were farm women, and they had no education in developing their sewing and cooking, and I think it was the most wonderful thing that ever happened. I feel like I've gotten a college education from the time I've worked with Extension. And think of all the women who got the same education that I did. I wouldn't take anything for the education and the nice times I have had through my association with Extension Homemakers."

The lessons and camaraderie provided by Purdue's home economics extension service led by Lella, along with the formation of Home Economics Clubs, gave farm women a confidence never experienced before. Home economics knowledge gave rural women power over their daily lives, their homes, their children's futures, and their communities.

Dean Emeritus Eva Goble, who grew up on a farm in Clay County, Indiana, said, "The land-grant college was a different step because it said, 'Farm women—you're just as good as anybody else.' I can remember when my mother would hesitate to go to town because she thought the town women laughed at her, at what she was wearing or what she bought. Whatever she did, she felt they made fun of her. She didn't like it. Well, there's no farm woman today who would think that."

〜〜〜

As the Home Economics Clubs evolved and organized, they developed their own names and many began to make program books that listed a year's worth of lessons. At first they were written by hand. Some were a simple piece of paper folded over in book form. Sometimes a member would design and draw an image for the cover. Later the program book was typed and included the Club's chosen color and flower, a creed and prayer, along with the roster of local and county officers. Clubs were named after women or local landmarks, including the town or county in which the club resided. Many names had a spunky ring. There was the Sugar Creek Club, Merry Moms Club, Peppy Peppers Club, Good Will Club, Busy Bee Club, and the Polly Anna Club, among thousands of others. Yet with all of the creative names, when women headed out their doors, they said to their families, "I'm going to Club."

Achievement Day was the pinnacle of the year. It was an all-day meeting held at a church, school, or other large venue. Each club exhibited examples from the lessons they had been taught over the year. First, second, and third place ribbons were awarded. Often, four hundred to six hundred women attended Achievement Day dressed in their finest, donning hats and gloves.

Fair exhibits were also a highlight. Each Club entered in as many divisions as they could, for each ribbon earned points for the group. All the points were added together and the Club with the highest score won. In *Going to Club*, Martha Whitehead, age seventy-two, shared a memory of the Boone County Fair:

> Years ago we had the women's exhibits in what was then the Armory. Miss Lella Gaddis was going to judge for the show and she came to us and said they just didn't hardly have any canning and would I hunt up something that I could exhibit. So Wilbur and I went down into the basement and we picked out a can of yellow wax beans and a can of red cherries because we thought they looked kind of good together. . . . and I got a blue ribbon on them. When Wilbur found out about it, he kind of exploded. 'You can't accept that; you're the County Agent's wife.' Miss Gaddis said, 'You will accept it, because I didn't know whose it was when I placed it.' So the first year I lived here, and the first time I ever exhibited anything, I got a blue ribbon.

Purdue's short courses and conferences were special events for women of Indiana's Home Economics Clubs. Mary Matthews and Virginia Meredith had established the Indiana Home Economics Association (IHEA) in 1913, and each year afterward, women attended Purdue Home Economics Conferences originally held for a week in January. It was an opportunity for women to learn and meet people and experience a university campus, often for the first time. In 1980, Pearl McCall, age ninety, of Daviess County remembered attending a 1922 Purdue short course. She said:

> That's how I got enthused with chickens. They had incubators, and I had never seen an incubator. I come home and I bought two or three. I could put 110 eggs in there. . . . All that was new to me. . . . we had a session on planning and planting a garden and the different varieties of vegetables that you could raise and how much you ought to plant for the size family you had . . . and it was all worked out on paper that you could bring home with you. Of course you couldn't hope to remember all that, so that was awfully nice of them.

Both Mary Mathews and Lella Gaddis spoke at Purdue Home Economics Conferences. Alma Knecht, age seventy-eight, of Wabash County said, "I was down at Purdue, and Lella Gaddis gave a talk one day while we were there. I got to talk with her privately. At that time, we were wearing two-piece suits, and I asked her what kind of clothes to buy. She said, 'Alma, buy a good suit when you buy one, and don't buy anything that is shabby to begin with, because it doesn't last.' So I remember that."

In the early days, professors such as Mary Matthews opened their homes to the women attending the Home Economics Conferences, serving them meals and treating them with great hospitality. Meals were also served in the Home Economics Cafeteria, which was a new experience for many women. Margaret Butler, age eighty-seven, of Steuben County said, "And we could go to the cafeteria and get what we wanted. They had everything. Seemed to me like it was a party every day. I remember some of the things we had to eat—things I had never had in my life—tomato aspic . . . and dessert in little patty shells. I still got some of the recipe sheets I brought home from those first meetings. I kept them all these years. I get them out and look at them every once in awhile."

From 1905 to 1947, Agricultural Extension exhibit trains hit the rails to reach many people quickly and focus attention on specific educational needs. Many railroads provided the trains at no cost to Purdue University. This mode of transportation was referred to as "The Traction," and it wove a pattern of rails like a spider web over Indiana, with the center of the web at Indianapolis. Before good roads and automobiles, there was The Traction. Between Christmas and New Year's Day in 1905, the first Purdue extension train in Indiana visited eighty-two stations along the Lake Erie and Western railroad, with George Christie giving a lesson on corn judging. Eventually, all departments offered lectures and demonstrations on traction exhibit or "demonstration" trains.

Farmers, their sons, and eventually their wives and mothers waited at the depots ahead of scheduled times. Politicians were warned that they could attend but could not use the exhibit stops for campaigning purposes. People came in droves to the "Alfalfa Train," "Dairy Train," and "Wheat Train." The "B & O Soybean Special" train offered demonstrations on the best use of soybeans in cooking. A stove, demonstration counter, and blackboard were installed in the boxcar, and seats were provided for the women who watched in the wintertime wearing coats and hats. The clang of the bell, black smoke from the stack of the coal-burning engines, and the hiss of the steam beckoned rural Indiana people to learn and better their farms and lives with lessons from Purdue University. Lella packed her bags and taught on some of the trains.

At the 1920 annual meeting of the IHEA held at Purdue, Director of the Department of Agricultural Extension George Christie presented a plan to run a Home Special Train in Indiana and suggested that the association back the project. Lella was on board, literally, and Kate makes record in her diary:

Aneta Beadle Vogler of Purdue University and her 4-H helper Mary Mowry demonstrate how to cook with soybeans on the B & O Soybean Special Train that traveled through the corn belt of Ohio, Indiana, and Illinois in 1941. They prepared soybean loaf, soybean muffins, and soy fudge and served the foods to the women in attendance. J.C. Allen Collection, Going to Club, Eleanor Arnold. Courtesy of Purdue University Libraries, Archives and Special Collections.

March 14: Went over to see Home Improvement Train.

March 15: Lella went on the Home Improvement Train for the week.

April 17: The train gets back from its five-week trip.

The exhibit trains made a huge impact on the lives of Indiana people as they experienced challenging times. The demonstration trains chugged through the state during both World Wars, the 1918 flu epidemic, and the Great Depression. During the forty-two years the rolling exhibits existed, 408,137 Hoosiers visited 1,440 station stops. The hospitality of the railroad workers and the eager, knowledgeable Purdue staff won the hearts of the people. During tough times, Purdue people cared and wanted to help, and when the train arrived at the nearest station, farm folk came running to board.

The final "Farm and Home Special" ran in March of 1947. It was a "sign-off" train that beheld demonstrations of all the latest in agricultural and home economics science to date. It consisted of eight coaches with twenty-three exhibits and two sleeping cars and a dining car for Purdue staff. The railroads' important role in the development of agriculture and home economics extension ended that spring with the Farm and Home Special tooling down the tracks.

Purdue's radio station WBAA first went on the air in 1934. A one-hour program featured various organizations. One week, the program highlighted Home Economics Clubs in an effort to increase membership. In *Going to Club*, Mildred McCay, age eighty-five, of Tippecanoe County remembered that day:

> Our county agent thought it would be nice if a group of home ec women would get together and rehearse a little bit with Al Stewart (Director of Purdue Musical Organizations) and sing something on that program. . . . So, when it came time for the program, why, we sang on the radio. It must have been great. I've thought about it so many times. I've laughed when I think how that must have sounded, with just one little practice.

The Indiana Home Demonstration Chorus directed by Al Stewart, of Purdue Musical Organizations, grew from thirty-two original members in 1934 to nearly 4,500 members throughout the state. It became the largest women's chorus in the world. In this image, they are performing in the Hall of Music at Purdue University. Courtesy of Purdue University Libraries, Archives and Special Collections.

That day the Tippecanoe County Home Demonstration Chorus was born. The thirty-two original members spurred the organization of Home Demonstration Choruses throughout Indiana. The county chorus idea spread rapidly, and in 1937, music was made a part of the Agricultural Extension Service with the appointment of Albert P. Stewart as state leader to establish and supervise statewide participation. An annual festival was held at Purdue with as many as 3,000 singers performing in Purdue's Hall of Music. The Indiana Home Demonstration Chorus had 4,500 total members and was the largest organized women's chorus in the world.

Also in 1934, there were plans to start a National Home Economics Association. Lora Herrick of Cass County was sent to Washington, DC to represent Purdue at an organizational meeting. "Each state had something special they got up and talked about," she said. "My subject was music because we had a chorus in Indiana, which no one else had.

We had a wonderful state leader, Al Stewart, and we had this great big chorus, so I was to tell about Indiana being the singing state."

The Indiana Home Demonstration Chorus was the first amateur group to sing at the Hollywood Bowl as a benefit to the "Crippled Children of Los Angeles." Helen Weigle of Tippecanoe County remembered the event: "We all came and had our concert in the Hall of Music [at the Purdue Conference], and while we were singing, the Glee Club boys were loading our luggage. When the concert was over, we got on the train and started for California."

The Chorus traveled to Canada to sing in the International Exhibition in front of thirty thousand people. They sang in nine European countries. They sang the poems of Indiana's James Whitcomb Riley to thousands attending the Sesquicentennial Celebration in Washington, DC. They performed a "Hoosier Holiday" in Sarasota, Florida, and thousands heard them sing at the Portland, Oregon Rose Festival. The first performers wore black robes; later the robes were a rainbow of colors.

Hazel Dolkey from Knox County said, "I remember one time we sang in Indianapolis for President Eisenhower. All 2,000 of us sang in a body. We sang 'The Lord's Prayer,' and on our way back, our bus driver said, 'I have heard "The Lord's Prayer" sang many times, but I never heard it as pretty as it was sung tonight.'"

In 1936, they gave an impromptu performance at the White House. Mildred McCay was there and remembered, "Our Indiana Homemakers Chorus was invited to sing at the opening session of the ACWW [Associated Country Women of the World] meeting in Washington, D.C. . . . I heard Mrs. Roosevelt ask if our chorus would come to the White House and sing for the President at the lawn party that afternoon. Of course, we were so thrilled about that."

The chorus decided to sing "Home on the Range," one of President Franklin Roosevelt's favorite tunes. Afterward, Mrs. Roosevelt walked the lawn filled with thousands of women and shook as many hands as she could.

❦

Today the Association started by Virginia Meredith and Mary Matthews in 1913 is called the Indiana Extension Homemakers Association (IEHA). Through the years women of the Association have provided thousands of "covered dishes" to "shut-ins," the sick, and the bereaved. They have collected for the American Red Cross and the Salvation Army and sponsored polio shots for families. Women of IEHA have begun hot lunch programs in schools, started kindergarten classrooms, and held summer camps for low-income children. They have visited the mentally ill, made dolls for little girls in hospitals, established college scholarships for young women, and baked thousands of cookies for thousands of fund-raisers, schoolchildren, soldiers, and lost souls. In the early years, the Association endorsed the Indiana Library Commission to promote libraries for rural areas. In 1923, the women of Association were well ahead of their time when the group endorsed a movement for the prevention of smoking in public places. The 1950s brought programs on citizenship, government, safety, health, and the "role of women in the changing world."

In the early years, Mary was on the executive committee of IEHA three times and was president from 1917 to 1919. Lella was not made an officer until 1941 when she was named honorary president, a position she held until 1959.

While American life has changed dramatically since the IEHA was founded, still today the woman is the heart of the family. She is the one nurturing each family member's wellbeing and creating a home that is a safe haven. Time and technology will never change that designation. Now she may not raise chickens or make cottage cheese, but she is eager to know the latest studies in nutrition. She may not sew winter coats for her children, but she is still responsible for providing those coats. The woman is still the one taking macaroni and cheese to a sick neighbor and providing the cookies for the bake sale, even if they are store-bought. The aspirations of the IEHA have not changed since its beginning. In 2010, the Association's Web site stated, "It is the mission of the Indiana Extension Homemakers Association to strengthen families through continuing education, leadership development, and volunteer community support." When the Association began in 1913, there were fifty-eight members. The peak of membership occurred in the 1950s when there were 2,745 clubs with 66,798 women. In 2009, there were 993 clubs with 11,969 members.

In 1930, Mrs. C. W. Horne of Hendricks County, a dressmaker and designer of women's apparel, won a contest to write a creed for the Association. Since then, the creed has been memorized and repeated by thousands of women in Home Economics Clubs across Indiana. It is still the creed utilized today:

Home Demonstration Creed

We believe in the present and its opportunities, in the future and its promises, in everything that makes life large and lovely, in the divine joy of living and helping others, and so we endeavor to pass on to others that which has benefited us, striving to go onward and upward, reaching the pinnacle of economic perfection, in improving, enlarging and endearing the greatest institution in the world—The Home.

Good of the Union

Indiana's laws required the teaching of "domestic science" in the seventh and eighth grades of grammar schools for the first time in the late 1910s. Purdue University appointed Mary Matthews to establish a summer school for teachers who lacked training to teach this subject. Kate Gaddis attended these summer school sessions. Both men and women teachers took the study courses prepared by Mary. In 1921, Little, Brown and Company of Boston published a textbook written by Mary for use in the seventh and eighth grade classroom. It was entitled *Elementary Home Economics—First Lessons in Sewing and Textiles, Foods and Cookery, and the Care of the House.* The book was highly successful, as it was the only textbook adopted in Indiana for the teaching of seventh and eighth grade domestic science classes for more than twenty years. The tan, leather-bound book with etchings of two little girls— one cooking and the other in sewing class—was revised five times.

In the book's preface written on her thirty-eighth birthday, October 13, 1920, Mary wrote, "While there are a number of textbooks on Home Economics for the elementary schools, there seems to be a need for one dealing with more than one phase of the subject as it is now taught in these schools. This book is intended for use in schools where one book is desired to cover the entire course, and is strictly an elementary treatment of the subject."

Perhaps after compiling photographs, drawings, swatches of fabric, recipes, and writing 343 pages of text, Mary chose to write the preface to her book on the day of her birth as a celebratory gift to herself. While writing and gathering information, she had been busy with many other endeavors. She had just opened the first Practice House. She was developing the Department of Household Economics and the Indiana Home Economics Association. The planning and construction of the new Home Economics Building was taking place. In addition, at this time, as if a book, new building, students, staff, and faculty responsibilities were not enough, she did her part to fend off prowlers by loaning Vern Freeman her Smith and Wesson.

Mary also wrote *The House and Its Care*, the first book in the field, which she revised three times, and she authored *Clothing, Selection and Care*. She was a contributing author for *The Book of Rural Life, 1925*, writing the section on "House Furnishing." Mary was surprised by the popularity of *Elementary Home Economics* and once said, "My royalties amounted to more than my salary, but of course salaries were small then, and I had little competition for there were only a few home economics books to be had." On the back of a 1924 edition of *Elementary Home Economics* are the words, "The price marked hereon is fixed by the state, and any deviation therefrom should be reported to the State Superintendent of Public Instruction. Retail price, $1.26. Exchange price, 98-cents."

Also in 1921 as faculty advisor, Mary piloted the founding of the Indiana Delta Chapter of Pi Beta Phi Fraternity at Purdue. Even though Pi Beta Phi is an organization for women, it is officially a fraternity, not a sorority. The word "sorority" had not been coined in 1867 when Pi Beta Phi was founded at Monmouth College in Monmouth, Illinois. Mary supervised the financing of a chapter house referred to in 1944 as "the finest on the campus." From 1927 to 1939, the Pi Beta Phi house was located on Littleton Street. Then the house was moved to its current location at 1012 State Street. Because of Mary's staunch friendship and hospitality to both the actives and alumnae, the library in the chapter house was named the "Mary Lockwood Matthews Library," and a bookplate was designed in her name.

Mary was president of the Pi Beta Phi Alumnae Association for twenty-five years and was hailed as "Indiana Delta's First Lady."

Mary worked hard, she read a great deal, she wrote, and she lectured. She kept up to date. She was a seasoned speaker and spoke before many audiences at Purdue, on the radio, and before extension groups. She graciously entertained in the home she shared with her mother, hosting Purdue people, visitors to campus, and her neighbors. Yet she admitted that she did not like to cook, even though she had cooked a great deal in her lifetime, especially when she prepared meals for threshers when she lived on a farm with her mother. In a 1944 article in *The Economist*, Mary was quoted as saying, "I like to sew, but scarcely have time to mend my clothes. I like to write, but time is limited for that, also; I am very fond of housekeeping and homemaking, and I like to have people in for meals and have always enjoyed entertaining both faculty and students—that is, until rationing went into effect, and my good maid after fifteen years, left me."

President Stone's death was a national sensation and the university community was in shock. Before rescuers had reached President Stone's body in the Canadian Rockies, the Purdue University Board of Trustees met to appoint recent board member Henry Wright Marshall as vice president of the University and, subsequently, acting president until Stone's successor was found. Marshall was the publisher of the Lafayette *Journal and Courier* and had extensive farming experience. He also was a politician who had served six years in the Indiana General Assembly. His business experience was what the board was looking for when they made him acting president. Marshall stayed in the background handling the University's business affairs, while "Grand Old Man" Dean of Men Stanley Coulter presided as chairman of the faculty and handled academic needs. Both men also assisted in the search for a new president.

When Virginia Meredith became a member of the Purdue University Board of Trustees in July of 1921, there were three thousand students on campus. She brought to the group her desire for the University to do more for women than it had in the previous fifty years. Two months later, the death of Professor A. M. Kenyon, head of the Department of Mathematics, left an opening on the faculty's executive committee and an opportunity for more representation for women. Coulter gave Marshall a list of five names of candidates he knew could ably serve on the committee and replace Kenyon. Included on that list was the name of one woman, Mary Matthews. Marshal selected Matthews to fill the vacancy, which was both a career accomplishment and personal joy for her mother Virginia. Marshall said he appointed Mary "because the Home Economics Department has no direct representation in the Executive Committee as now organized. As a further reason for this appointment, there has been but one woman member of the Committee and fourteen men. I feel that because of the large number of women students, there should be two women on the Executive Committee."

In April 1922, the trustees unanimously elected Edward Charles Elliott to become the sixth president of Purdue University. Elliott was forty-seven when he came to Purdue from the University of Montana where he had been chancellor. Elliott's charisma, savvy, and administrative talents would move Purdue into a new realm, and he would become an ally for Mary Matthews. When Elliott and his family moved from Helena to Lafayette the summer of 1922, the University did not have a home for the new president. Mrs. Elliott was concerned about the size of house Purdue would provide. The Elliotts had four children ranging in age from seven to fourteen. In addition, Mrs. Elliott's mother, Mrs. Nowland, lived with the Elliotts. Temporary housing was provided in a house at 500 University Street, north of the Purdue Armory. (The house no longer exists.) The trustees discussed constructing a new presidential home on campus, but the Elliotts were not keen on living a fishbowl existence. Then in 1923, the trustees decided to purchase a home owned by Dr. Guy Levering at 515 South 7th Street, on a bluff overlooking downtown Lafayette. The rambling stucco home cost $44,000 and was located across the Wabash River, away from campus life. It stood across the street from the home of Purdue University Trustee David E. Ross.

The distance from President Elliott's home to his office was about two miles. Daily, Elliott walked out his door on South 7th Street, down the tree-lined hill, through the Lafayette business district, across the Main Street Bridge, over the Wabash, and up the steep rise of State Street to the campus. Friends motoring by offered him rides, but he would turn them away, for he enjoyed the walks as a substitute for the days when he and his sons hiked the Montana mountains.

When Elliott arrived at Purdue he discovered that his predecessor, Stone, had personally authorized every invoice and every payment from University funds. He had done most of the bookkeeping and business processing himself. Under Stone's watch, the only business office the University had was a bookkeeper-secretary named Edward Augustus Ellsworth, whose title was bursar. Immediately, Elliott began to change Purdue's financial ways, for he had no interest in keeping such a tight thumb on every dollar. He had a University to lead. He hired William T. Middlebrook as controller and within his office centered all University financial operations except those of the Agricultural Experiment Station and Extension Service. Once on the job, Middlebrook learned that the University's funds were in more than 125 separate bank accounts. He immediately established a double-entry bookkeeping system. Elliott also learned that Stone not only controlled the bookkeeping himself, but he also carried keys to every lock on the campus. The new president had no interest in bothering with the day-to-day mundane nuances of the University and a bevy of keys jangling around in his pocket, so the controller was assigned those duties. Then Elliott was free to accomplish his aspirations for Purdue University.

After three years, Middlebrook left for the University of Minnesota, and R. B. Stewart, one of Purdue's most influential university administrators, arrived on the scene. Stewart's presence heralded the arrival of solid business practices for Purdue and another mentor for Mary Matthews and the School of Home Economics.

When Virginia Meredith became a trustee in 1921, she was off and running with each turn of events and the launching of her dreams for women at Purdue. With President Stone's death soon after her appointment, her daughter named to the faculty's executive committee, and her work to build a women's residence hall, she added another monumental task to juggle at that time. Virginia became a principal in the design, construction, financing, and management of the Purdue Memorial Union. She believed in the idea of erecting a building dedicated to the more than four thousand alumni who had served in the Civil War and World War I. The Purdue Memorial Union Association was formed with a leadership body known as the board of governors, and three of its members were selected from the board of trustees: Virginia Meredith, Joseph Oliver, and David Ross. Virginia was named president of the Purdue Memorial Union Association board of governors, just two months after being named to the board of trustees.

The first push to build a student union on campus began in 1912 with a fund-raising drive. The members of the 1912 senior class and the seniors that followed them were asked to donate five dollars each to help finance the Purdue Memorial Union building. These funds were given to the board of trustees for safekeeping until enough money was raised. World War I put the fund-raising campaign on hold, and when the war ended, the initial concept of constructing a building for students evolved into creating a building to memorialize Purdue's veterans, and that's where Virginia came in.

Throughout the 1920s, raising money to build the Purdue Memorial Union turned out to be an ongoing, agonizing process. The original plan called for the building to be financed by private donations and built on state-owned, University-controlled property. Those paying a pledge of $100 or more toward the building fund would hold a special distinction. They would become life members of the Purdue Memorial Union Association, and their names would be inscribed in bronze and displayed on the main floor of the building. (The large bronze plaque with a patina darkened by time still graces the hallway near the Great Hall.) Pledges from students, alumni, and others poured in from around the country.

On June 13, 1922, with a bright look to the future, Virginia led the groundbreaking for the building. She introduced fellow Purdue University Trustee David Ross, who turned over the first spade of dirt, while the project contractor, A. E. Kemmer, dug the first furrow. Minutes before the first spade of dirt was realized and the groundbreaking ceremony began, Virginia gazed down upon the ground where she stood at the southeastern edge of the campus in the future building's prominent and visible spot, and she found a four-leaf clover. Virginia bent and plucked the symbol of good luck from the Purdue soil. She kept the clover safely with her, and later, it was framed with a caption recording the day. The leafy charm is preserved today in the Purdue University Virginia Kelly Karnes Archives and Special Collections Re-

On June 13, 1922, Virginia Meredith led the groundbreaking for the construction of the Purdue Memorial Union. Minutes before David Ross turned over the first spade of dirt, Virginia gazed upon the ground and found a four-leaf clover. One can envision the good luck charm in its gleaming gold frame, hanging on the wall of the home Virginia shared with her daughter Mary Matthews on Waldron Street in West Lafayette, Indiana. Courtesy of Purdue University Libraries, Archives and Special Collections.

search Center. Little did Virginia know, it would take eight years of struggle for the Purdue Memorial Union to be completed.

Construction began in 1922, but a year later the board of governors ran out of money. To everyone's shock, donors were not honoring their commitments to pay off their pledges. The board feared the building would become an eyesore if funds were not available, and the building had to be boarded up and left in construction limbo. Trustees David Ross and Henry Marshall borrowed a large amount of money to roof the building before winter set in. Without their benevolent gift, the building would have been left to deteriorate in the elements.

The Purdue Memorial Union was still not finished when the doors opened for the first time in September 1924. Opening before its completion allowed the Association to begin generating revenue. On opening day, the main level had temporary pine floors, and the walls and ceiling were not yet plastered. The second floor was incomplete. The cafeteria was open on the ground floor and could serve one thousand people per meal. A weekly meal ticket cost $4.50.

Lella and Kate Gaddis were part of the opening festivities, and were some of the first to attend functions there. Kate writes:

> September 9: Went to the opening supper last night at the Student Union Building. They seem to be in debt.
>
> October 3: The first University Women's Club at the Student Union Building.

Dean of Women Carolyn Shoemaker was a major supporter of the Purdue Memorial Union and in the initiative to raise funds for its construction. After her death, it was learned that she gave $5,000 of her own resources for the drive.

Even after a letter was sent in 1925 politely but firmly requesting donors make good on their pledges, not all payments were made in full. By January 1927, President Elliott was inclined to take those who did not pay to court, and he asked for advice from the University's legal counsel, Allison E. Stuart. However, the cost of each lawsuit and the bad press it would incur among the Purdue alumni made going to court an unsuitable solution. By 1929, the board of trustees and the

Purdue Memorial Union Association voted to allow the board of trustees full control of the project. On January 8, 1930, the Purdue Memorial Union was finally complete and operational. Virginia Meredith was eighty years old when she first walked on the terrazzo tile, relished the regal woodwork, and saw the sunlight shine through the soft pastel stained glass windows of the ballrooms.

One of the first clubs to meet in the Purdue Memorial Union before it was complete was the Purdue Women's Club. Professor Laura Anna Fry, head of the Art Department for more than thirty years, persuaded Mrs. Stanley Coulter, wife of the Dean of Men, to call a meeting of the women on the campus. About 125 women first met in the library on March 16, 1922, to discuss "an organization that would promote sociability among the women of the university circle." Mary Matthews and Lella Gaddis were among the charter members. According to the minutes, when the first meeting adjourned, "Homemade candy was passed while the women visited a little while." Membership in the club was popular from its beginning as an answer to a need felt by faculty women and wives to retain the personal quality of their friendships as the staff of the University grew in number. While there was the University Club for faculty members and their spouses, it did not satisfy women's desires for close relationships, so the Purdue Women's Club was created. Membership dues were fifty cents a year. Names for the club were discussed. Those rejected included Purdue Faculty Ladies, Faculty Women's Club, and Frolicsome Faculty Females. The simple dignity of the name Purdue Women's Club won hearts.

Early member, Miss Miller, said of the club's start, "We did not cut much figure at first. We did not even get a notice in the *Exponent* that spring for any of our three meetings. But the very day we organized, a university jersey cow named Estella made the front page in a big headline for receiving a silver cup for producing the greatest amount of milk."

In the beginning, meetings were held in the Library, and as attendance increased, the women met in Ladies Hall, more often called the Art Building. One of the initial tasks of the club's secretary was to send a message of greeting from the new club to Mrs. Edward Elliott, wife of Purdue's new president. The club's first meeting in the new

Purdue Memorial Union was on October 3, 1924. Mary Matthews was vice president at the time. (Lella Gaddis would be elected vice president of the Purdue Women's Club in 1949, two years after her retirement as state leader of home demonstration.) Lella and her sister Kate attended the fall meeting.

The women who attended the first meeting held at the Purdue Memorial Union were said to display "expressions of delight and appreciation of the privilege of having for the occasion a setting so beautiful and artistic in every respect as the Assembly room of the new building, and the hope that we might find it possible to meet there often."

However, in order to secure the Assembly Room, it was required that refreshments be ordered from the Union kitchen. Club members enjoyed creating their own refreshments and menus, so often they held their meetings in the Home Economics Building, which was also brand new. Yet for large gatherings, the Purdue Women's Club found the elegance of the Union to be the perfect setting.

In 1925, the immediate past president of the Purdue Women's Club, Mrs. Edward Elliott, wife of the president, offered her stately home on South 7th Street in Lafayette for the October tea honoring new members. Throughout her life, Mrs. Elliott so fully supported and encouraged the club's activities that upon her death in 1955, the club established a scholarship fund in honor of the lady of "quiet, gentle character and cultured manner, impeccably dressed, often in blue with hat and gloves to complete her costume." Mrs. Elliott set a precedent in opening her home for the newcomers' tea that was followed by Priscilla Hovde, wife of President Frederick Hovde.

Ethel Christie was one of the first club presidents. She was Lella and Kate's good friend and the wife of the Director of the Agricultural Experiment Station George Christie. She sent out a "mimeographed" letter to possible members in September 1926 that read in part:

> This letter is to introduce to you the Purdue Women's Club, which was organized by the women of the university faculty to promote better acquaintance and good fellowship among Purdue women. . . . the officers and members of the Council of the Club will receive the women of the university in the Memorial Union building, from two-thirty to five 'o clock in the afternoon.

This is a photo of Dean Mary L. Matthews from Purdue University's 1932 Debris yearbook. That year, Mary was named chairman of the Department of Education by the Indiana Federation of Clubs, a post she held for twenty years. She was said to have a "selfless devotion to the cause of child welfare." Perhaps her own adoption prompted her to work for the betterment of children. Courtesy of Purdue University Libraries, Archives and Special Collections.

Two hundred women gathered for the October 1926 meeting in their white gloves and fashions of the Jazz Age. The program for the year promised "a future of friends, study, entertainment, music and drama . . . brilliant social coups and charming little speeches."

In 1930, Dean Mary Matthews was president of the club. Inspired by her conviction that "wives should keep up with their husbands intellectually," Mary initiated a meeting format that still exists today called "interest groups." Over the years, dozens of varied interest groups have focused on art, antiques, athletics, archery, bridge, current events, dramatics, gardening, home economics, music, needlecraft, literature, newcomers, typing, and more. The interest group is Mary's legacy to the Purdue Women's Club.

Also while president, Mary caused some friction in the club when she wanted to restrict membership to professional women only. She did not achieve her aim. A particular strength of the club has always been its determination to keep membership open to women in all areas of Purdue and to hold true to its original goal "to promote sociability among the women of the university."

Programs for general club events often focused on children, flowers, and fashion. In the early years, club members were invited to Mrs. Christie's garden to watch children perform a May dance. In 1935, the Garden Groups arranged a rainbow of flowers around Purdue University Trustee Virginia Meredith as she gave a speech defining the mission of the club as building loyalty to the school. Four hundred guests applauded a play in 1935 that depicted two hundred years of womanhood. The cast acted out what they thought the year 1999 would be like with a man acting as a "husband-housekeeper" and a woman as an ultramodern wife. Later that year, Lillian Gilbreth, engineering consultant and professor of management, addressed the fall luncheon. She said, "The challenge of today's problems requires us to be peaceful within if we are to be peaceful outwardly . . . The big job for university women is to make others fit for life's adjustment, to help their families adjust themselves, and make them feel at ease in a confused world . . . It requires physical adequateness through rest and relaxation."

Today Gilbreth's words could be spoken at a meeting of the Purdue Women's Club, and women would nod their heads in agreement, as we still long for peace through rest and relaxation.

Friend Dave

As the 1920s approached, Lella and Kate were busy buying and selling property. They were doing very well financially for women of their day. They purchased a lot for $850 on the east side of Russell and 3rd Streets, across the street from their home. Kate said that "someday" they would build a house there. They also sold their former home on Salisbury and paid off their residence.

In July 1919, the sisters took a trip out west to Denver, Colorado, by automobile and visited friends and Kansas State Agriculture College. The roads at that time were merely glorified dirt paths filled with ruts and rocks, which made the ride a bouncy, dusty journey. The weather was quite hot during most of their traveling. Kate records:

> July 12: Drive to Hannibal and over the worst road I ever saw to Macon. A drive of 130 miles.

> July 17: Lie around and rest. Am reading "A Daughter of the Land." Ride and eat and sleep is about all we do.

> July 24: Went up the Moffitt Road. Such a wonderful ride. Made snowballs and gathered flowers.

Published in 1918, *A Daughter of the Land* was another book by Indiana author Gene Stratton-Porter. The story is uncanny in its parallels to some of Kate's life. In fact, the main character is named Kate. It is about a young girl who is a member of a large, prosperous farm family. The Kate in the book has been designated to be her mother's helper in her old age. She believes this is unfair, for her brothers have been given land and her older sisters are to be trained as teachers. With help of a nephew and sister-in-law, she becomes a teacher and leaves home. However, her true ambition is to own a large farm. She suffers through a bad marriage but ultimately acquires her land and is happy.

One can see Kate Gaddis, teacher, owner of three parcels of land and a fine house, with her eyeglasses perched on her nose, book in hand, sitting in a Model T that bumps past corn and wheat fields. No doubt, she reveled in *A Daughter of the Land*.

❦

As their money accumulated and their lives became more affluent, Lella and Kate were generous, especially if it meant helping their special nephew, the only child of their sister Mamie and her husband Reverend Henry Clay Riley. Kate writes on November 27, 1922, "Lella gets Paul a new overcoat. He is quite fond of it. Might as well help them now, as leave it to them."

Both Lella and Kate received yearly raises, and they were sought-after career women of the time. Other land-grant universities knew of Lella's good works, and they wanted to hire her. Kate was a highly recommended schoolteacher, as is evidenced in her diary notations:

> June 10, 1921: Get my contract $1,390 to be paid in 10 equal payments.

> June 25: Had an offer from Sevanton, Pa. to teach in Miss Fields Country Day School for $2000.

Michigan State University offered Lella a position paying $3,200 a year, but she turned it down. The previous year she had received a raise from Purdue and was earning $2,520. The same month that the search team recovered the body of President Stone and rescued his wife, Margaret, from a Canadian mountaintop, the Gaddis women bought another piece of land. This lot was south of where they lived and cost $1,000. Lella and Kate were planted and happy where they were. They had accumulated properties and fostered kinships with the men of the School of Agriculture and the wives and children of those men. Their family lived nearby. No job and no amount of money would entice these women to pull up roots and move away from Purdue University, West Lafayette, and the fine lives they were creating for themselves.

In the spring of 1922, the women began the construction of a house on their property across the street. They acted as their own contractors. Because Lella was traveling and school was out for summer break, Kate was the chief supervisor:

> August 25: We may be saving a contractors price, but it takes lots of calling up and fussing around.

> August 30: Lella left to be gone until Friday night. They sent pine treads instead of oak. We will not have them.

Once the house across the street was finished, Lella and Kate rented it to their good friends, Thomas and Julia Coleman. Thomas started at Purdue in 1913 as a county agent leader, and in 1920 he was named assistant director of Agricultural Extension. The Colemans had a daughter, also named Julia, and Kate cared for her often.

In the summer of 1920, Kate traveled with other teachers to New York City where she took classes at Columbia University. They took in the sights in their off time, visiting Broadway, art museums, China Town, Grant's "monument," and West Point. She writes:

> July 4: Took a trip to the Goddess of Liberty. This is some big city.

> July 6: Today we pay our tuition $62.00, $8 for each point and $6 extra. Went to our three classes.

> July 14: I went down to the City Library deposited $3 for a card. Now belong to N.Y. City Library.

> July 31: Took a trip to Atlantic City. It is so different from anything we ever had seen. The boardwalk and ocean.

Kate and her fellow teachers worked very hard during their six weeks at Columbia University, and she commented, "We are so busy we can't see for the dust we are making." She worried about taking home the credits she needed. It was in the dead of summer and the heat was intense, yet she said, "We have to pinch ourselves to believe we are here." While she was starstruck with the magic of New York City and enjoyed her occasional free time, she had a teacher who put a damper on things. Kate said that Miss Pennell did not like her paper as she read it out in class. Kate defended her work, writing, "It was a good paper." In another entry, she told of meeting Miss Pennell in the hallway, and the two women had "quite a talk." Kate described their encounter as, "We don't seem to hitch as to the work." The next month after Kate was home, she received her grades from Columbia—three B's and one D. She does not say the "D" was from Miss Pennell, but given their differences, it is quite probable.

Days after Kate cast her first vote in the 1920 November election, a sad and unnerving event occurred that Kate would have to face through the holiday season. On November 21, she received a ride home from church with a friend named Sam, and the car they were in collided with a coal car. A woman named Mrs. Lucas was killed.

> November 22: Had to go down to the coroner and testify. Poor Sam is crushed over the affair, and it is not his fault.
>
> December 14: Get an invitation from the Grand Jury to appear Thursday morning. I do hope they get this case settled.
>
> December 16: Go to the courthouse at nine. One juror does not come. Back at 3:30. My but I was frightened.
>
> December 17: The Grand Jury dismisses the case.
>
> December 18: I see by the paper that Sam is not going to drive an automobile.

Also that year, Kate became the legal guardian for the sisters' Aunt Beck who lived in Rossville. From her diaries, it sounds as if the family had to give their approval to have Kate handle her aunt's affairs and tending. She said, "Some of the relation are mad at me, but it is the best thing for Aunt Beck." Kate mentioned how confused Aunt Beck was and referred to her as "such a care" and "she does not know where she is." Kate was compassionate and loyal to her aunt, traveling to Rossville to pick her up and bring her to her home to visit. On October 15, 1922, Aunt Beck died of pneumonia. She was taken to the Gaddis sisters' home, and friends came to pay their respects. At the end of her diary, Kate summed up events of that year by saying, "Aunt Beck, poor old dear, gone to her reward. Relation find I have not cheated them or mistreated Aunt Beck. New House built. We thank God for health."

In the spring of that year, Lella became a charter member of the Altrusa Club in West Lafayette. Known today as Altrusa International, the organization was started in Nashville, Tennessee, by Dr. Alfred Durham, a member of the Kiwanis. After many women went to work during World War I, Durham envisioned the Altrusa Institutes. They would be a chain of national clubs where business and professional women could meet and exchange ideas. Then he met Mamie L. Bass of Indianapolis. She served as the women's division superintendent of the U.S. Employment Services and was a partner in her brother's architecture firm. While she admired Durham's Altrusa Institute, Bass felt that Altrusa could serve a higher purpose. In June 1918, when Altrusa held its first convention in Indianapolis, Bass's vision became a reality. She created the Principles of Altrusa, which defined Altrusa as "a builder of women" and an organization based on merit and accomplishment. The principles were officially adopted in 1921 along with a major campaign to establish more clubs. By 1922, Altrusa had 20 clubs, and one of those was the charter club to which Lella belonged. In 1925, Lella was elected state president of the Altrusa organization. The group became international in 1935 with the organization of its first club in Mexico. Since, it has expanded around the globe. According to the organization's Web site, today, Altrusa International is still "first and foremost, a grassroots organization that seeks to solve the problems in our back yards." They raise money for charities, volunteer at women's shelters, help runaway teens, build houses for Habitat for Humanity, and more. Bass said, "It is not enough to be good; Altrusans must be good for something."

In 1921, the sisters' nephew, Paul, was hired to do extension work in Purdue's poultry department. Two years later, he founded the Riley Poultry Farm at the north edge of West Lafayette at what today is Creighton Road. Kate records Paul's first egg purchases:

> March 3: Paul is setting 5700 eggs. One can hardly imagine such a lot. Hope he has good luck.
>
> March 26: Paul has 1500 little chicks and more hatching. We went out to see them yesterday.

By the end of April, Kate wrote of a job offer Paul received. Southwest Missouri State Teachers College (now known as Missouri State University) offered him a position paying $3,200. Kate said, "Not bad for a young man under thirty." Yet like his aunts, he did not accept the attractive offer and instead continued to build his poultry farm in West Lafayette. The following year almost to the day, Paul "set" 7,200 eggs and had "three shifts of them." In May, Lella and Kate drove out to his farm for eggs and mailed a boxful to a friend.

In the years to come, Paul would be recognized as one of the leading poultry breeders in the country. He was said to be ahead of his time and developed poultry concepts that were referred to in the industry as "Riley Methods." He was most famous for developing "Riley's Rapid Rocks." These chicks feathered rapidly after they lost their soft down, enabling the wait time for egg laying to be lessened. Paul's birds won many egg laying tests. His White Rock hen established a new world record for that breed in 1939-1940. He was also recognized for his business methods and in 1926 was hired as a district sales manager for Allied Mills, Inc., a commercial feed company in Chicago. Paul and Ruth's three children, whom Lella and Kate adored—Mary Louise, Robert, and Virginia—grew up helping with the chickens. Mary Louise said, "My brother, sister and I worked at whatever was needed to be done from the time we were children. Daddy told the story that we all learned to count by placing baby chickens from the incubators into the chick boxes."

Lella Gaddis is dressed in Colonial costume with members of the Purdue Women's Club in February, 1923. She stands third from the right on the steps of Ladies Hall. Laura Partch stands to Lella's right. In 1926, Mary Matthews enlisted Partch, who taught classes in home nursing and child care, to form the Purdue University Nursery School. Courtesy of Purdue University Libraries, Archives and Special Collections.

The year 1923 held many diverse experiences for Lella and Kate. They heard the new Purdue President Edward Elliott speak for the first time at Fowler Hall. Lella and Kate were invited to a reception at his home on South 7th Street. They attended meetings in the newly-opened Home Economics Building and ate in the cafeteria there for the first time. In February, Lella dressed in colonial costume for a Purdue Women's Club show to commemorate George Washington's birthday. Kate wrote in her diary that she and Lella saw Jackie Coogan in the silent film *Oliver Twist*. Coogan was a child actor who many years later became known as Uncle Fester on the 1960s sitcom *The Addams Family*.

There was disruption in the Lafayette school system where Kate taught. The city schools began the year without a superintendent. Also at the time, teachers were hoping for legislation to be passed that would provide them with a retirement fund. Kate makes a short and pointed statement about the turn of events on February 15, "Senate Bill on Retirement killed. Thanks."

A new superintendent was hired, but Kate's principal, Mrs. Taylor, did not like him. It turned out that she had good reason not to like him. The superintendent and school board members made frequent visits to Washington School, and then they lowered the boom. Kate writes:

> May 7: Notice in the paper that all the women principals are to be dropped. Someone seems very busy.
>
> May 10: Much school agitation. Don't know what will happen.
>
> May 18: The blow has fallen. All the women principals of the city schools dropped.

The headline to the story in the Lafayette *Journal and Courier* said, "WOMEN SCHOOL PRINCIPALS MAY LOSE POSITIONS, Board Known to Be Considering Plan to Dismiss them and Appoint Men in Their Place." The story does not say why the women were to be fired. However, a piece that ran the week before displayed this headline, "REPORT SHOWS DROP OF 361 IN SCHOOL PUPILS, Decrease Means Less Money."

Less money meant the need to cut costs and staff. Women were expendable back then. Men who supported families were thought to need jobs more than women who were supposed to get married and have a husband to support them. In 2010, Dean Emeritus Eva Goble said, "Women in 'Auntie' Kate's time couldn't even get teaching jobs a lot of times. They hired men first as teachers. They just wouldn't hire women."

The news story said, "If the board decides to remove the women principals, the order would affect some of the oldest and most highly esteemed educators in the grade schools of the city. Miss Mary Jefferson of Ford School has been engaged in the teaching profession for 50 years and is the dean of local school teachers."

The remainder of the school year played out with the women principals of the city "heartbroken." Kate was happy for the last day of school to arrive for all of the teachers were "very depressed" about Mrs. Taylor's firing.

> June 6: Have our Class Day. Principal in tears all the time.

> June 8: School is over and the last day for Mrs. Taylor. A sad last day. I had them all over for supper.

When Washington School reconvened the following fall, a new, young male principal had been hired. Kate described him as "wide awake." She liked him and his energy for the job. Kate displayed no hard feelings or animosity toward the replacement, even though she felt sad for her former principal. After thirty-five years of teaching at the age of fifty-five, Kate understood the politics involved in her position and the fact that women had little power. The one way Kate could foster camaraderie among her colleagues was to nurture them with dinner and hospitality. She served the outgoing principal and her fellow teachers—a subtle yet powerful action that brought the women together to support one another, even if they could not change the circumstances.

❧

By the end of 1923, Lella and Kate had paid off the new house they built across the street and rented to the Colemans. The next year they purchased their first car, a used sedan for which they paid $675. As she did many times a month, Kate traveled by train to Rossville in February to visit relatives, but her return was different from all those previous.

> February 23: Met at the train by H.J. [Reed] and Lella in the new car. Think of it—our car.

> March 15: Lella drives the car alone for the first time.

For several years, Lella had been driving cars across Indiana as the first state leader of home demonstration. Now she was sitting behind the wheel of her own automobile. Only twenty years earlier at the turn of the century, ideas prevailed that women were too timid and frail to handle complex machinery like an automobile. These same arguments were used to keep women from a higher education and the right to vote. However, there were women who were bold and courageous and drove anyway. In fact, in 1902, a woman named Mary Anderson invented the windshield wiper. Florence Lawrence, a silent film actress, invented the first turn signal and brake signal. In 1910, only 5% of licensed drivers were female. The invention of the self-starter in 1912 made way for more women drivers. It did away with the difficult and dangerous task of cranking an engine to start the car.

Two years before Lella and Kate purchased their automobile, Henry Ford opened his Phoenix Mill in Plymouth, Michigan, employing single or widowed women to do assembly and welding work. He would not hire married women. Ford said, "I consider women only a temporary factor in industry. Their real job in life is to get married, have a home and raise a family. I pay our women the same as men so they can dress attractively and get married."

Single, working, immaculately dressed Lella Reed Gaddis was forty-six when she drove her own car alone for the first time. It was a Chevrolet.

❧

In June of 1924, Kate wrote that Lella visited the country home of Purdue University Trustee and benefactor David Ross. She said the home was "lovely." He named his summer home "The Hills," located twelve miles southwest of campus. Today the area is a county park called Ross Hills Park with adjoining Ross Camp. Ross designed his three-story country home with a fireplace in the living room capped with a massive copper hood that directed heat to the upstairs. A wall of windows in this room gave a view of woods with trails that descended to the Wabash River. The house still stands at Ross Park. Ross also owned his city home on another hilltop at 506 South 7th Street in Lafayette, across the street from President Elliott's mansion. Today there is a vacant lot where Ross's city house once stood. Over the years, Lella would spend time at both of Ross's homes.

David Ross and George Ade, humorist, author, playwright, and
Purdue alumnus, had bought the sixty-five-acre Tilt Farm north of
campus, and gave money for the building of what is known today as
Ross-Ade Stadium. Both Ross and Ade were bachelors. Workers broke
ground on the stadium just weeks before Lella visited the country
home of David Ross. Ross-Ade Stadium was dedicated on November
22, 1924, during homecoming.

Ross had kind, puppy dog eyes and a friendly, open face. He was
loyal and devoted to his alma mater. He gave in so many extraordinary
ways to Purdue, his community, and to students. He gave to the Purdue Memorial Union, the Purdue Research Foundation, the Purdue
Airport, the Purdue Housing Research Campus, and the Ross Civil
Engineering Camp. The camp was developed in 1926 on land overlooking the Wabash River near his home where Lella visited. Ross
donated $50,000 toward the cost of Amelia Earhart's "flying laboratory," funding the Lockheed Electra Earhart flew from the Purdue

Lella Gaddis holds yeast bread baked as a "friendship wheel" by the Ruger Bakery Company of Lafayette, Indiana, for the Bakers Pageant in March 1928. The figures, as spokes in the wheel, represent the bakers of Indiana joined together in the State Association. This photograph was taken during the time Lella was seeing "Friend Dave" on a regular basis. Courtesy of Purdue University Libraries, Archives and Special Collections.

Airport in 1937 on her last flight. Ross was a Lafayette city councilman for eight years. He was known for his brief and pointed statements in any discussion. Lella, too, spoke her mind in a concise, matter-of-fact fashion, and she was devoted to Purdue and helping others. Lella and Ross were, in many ways, two of a kind. They were both dynamic, creative thinkers.

Lella continued to visit Ross's home and spend time with him on a regular basis as their busy schedules allowed, according to Kate's journal on August 9, 1926, "Lella goes out to Dave Ross's to meet his sister and spends the night."

This overnight visit was on the "up and up" with Ross's sister as chaperone. Miriam Epple-Heath, Lella's great-niece, said in 2010, "Lella and Dave Ross were very good friends. There was a feeling that I got indicating that they were enjoying each other's company. This was not generally known. One comment I heard from family was that Auntie Kate went along at one time or another to chaperone."

Ross was born near Brookston, Indiana. His father, a farmer, thought college was a waste of time. His uncle's persuasion changed his father's mind, and Ross was allowed to attend Purdue. He took electrical engineering classes. In his senior year, the *Exponent* said of Ross, "He will electrify Brookston." Later, Ross did help provide the first telephone service to Brookston as a founder of the Prairie Telephone Company. However, he would spark so much more. He was described as an "inventive genius." Ross would go on to patent three different mechanisms for automobiles and a number of patentable steering gears. The gear would change his personal course and the course of Purdue University. In 1906, the Ross Gear and Tool Company was founded, now part of TRW Commercial Steering. He refused an offer from Henry Ford that would have made his Ross Gear and Tool Company the sole supplier of steering gears for all Ford cars and trucks. Ross also started a research company devoted to the development of synthetic stone for building material. Rostone Corporation was founded in 1927. Ross's company blended shale, lime, alkaline, and soil to make a inexpensive "imitation stone" that could be made into slabs for outside veneer walls. It looked and felt like solid rock. Eventually, Ross received eighty-eight patents, mostly related to automobile steering, Rostone, and other building materials. He said, "There's scarcely a thing we do that can't be done better." One could imagine hearing Lella Gaddis utter the same sentiment as she held a home demonstration for Indiana women.

In her journals, Kate referred to David Ross as "Friend Dave." Lella and Friend Dave went horseback riding, golfing, and saw "picture shows" together. Yet there were few mentions of Ross visiting the Gaddis home or of the two attending public events together. Lella and Ross spent time alone in private pursuits. Perhaps they did not want Purdue people to talk of their "friendship."

The year after the Gaddis sisters bought their first pre-owned Chevrolet, they traded it in for a brand new 1926 model. They also built their third house on their latest property acquisition. Again, Kate handled the logistics of the build, and she kept a log of the construction in her diary. They began plans for the house in February, and by the end of summer, the house was built and ready for renters. In the midst, Kate writes about a medical problem:

> May 7: Went to see Dr. Arnett about my nose. Wait almost 2 hours.
>
> August 4: Went over to Dr. Eikins and had my nose burned with radium. Does not hurt but looks pretty bad.
>
> August 18: My nose is nasty and sore looking.
>
> September 10: Am so worried about my nose. Go to see the Dr.

Kate did not mention her nose again until the end of the following year when she wrote, "Of course, if I wanted to, I could worry about my nose, but I am not going to until I have to." Perhaps Kate underwent nasopharyngeal radium irradiation (NRI). This treatment was given to shrink swollen lymphoid tissue near the back of the nose. Through the 1960s, NRI was considered good medical practice and effective treatment for a number of medical problems of the head and neck, such as hearing loss and chronic ear infections, and for reducing the size of tonsils and adenoids. NRI treatment consisted of inserting two cylinders of radioactive radium sulfate through the nostrils into the space behind the nose and mouth for short lengths of time. Low doses of gamma radiation were delivered to the pituitary, thyroid, and salivary glands, and to the brain. Worldwide studies have not confirmed a definite link between NRI exposure and any disease, including cancer. Given that later Kate suffered with thyroid problems, including a goiter, along with diabetes, one may wonder if her radium treatment in 1926 had a bearing on the health problems she would have later in life.

Kate writes of Jazz Age diversions and history-making events in her 1927 diary:

March 23: Went to see "Gentlemen Prefer Blonds," a nasty, vulgar show. No place for a lady.

April 14: Went to see Will Rogers in the evening.

May 20: Our American boy Chas. Lindberg sailed across the ocean to Paris in 33 hours.

It is telling that Kate wrote "sails" rather than "flies" across the ocean. Flying was so new, the vernacular was not yet part of her everyday language.

Soon to turn fifty the following month, Lella was initiated into Alpha Chi Omega in April. An article in Alpha Chi Omega's *The Lyre* magazine said, "We are very proud to have initiated Miss Lella Gaddis, and to claim her as a member of Alpha Chi Omega. She is very prominent here at Purdue, being head of the extension department of home economics. She is very well known all over the state, and we feel she will do her share in bringing honor to Alpha Chi Omega."

In midlife, Lella enjoyed the company of a fine gentleman friend and an exhilarating career. New and inspiring personal and professional events unfurled with each turn of the calendar page.

Progress

Home economics was bestowed its own school when it separated from the School of Science in 1926. That was when Mary Matthews became the first dean of the School of Home Economics. Ironically, the school's name has changed twice in the years to follow, and both names have included the word "science." The school was renamed Consumer and Family Sciences in 1976, the same year the Home Economics Building was renamed Matthews Hall in honor of Mary. After a stint of thirty-four years as the School of Consumer and Family Sciences, the department is now part of the College of Health and Human Sciences, established in 2010. Today's students may walk past Matthews Hall unaware of its history, but Mary's mark is in the foundation of the building and the roots of the new college.

In the 1926 annual report of the University, President Edward Elliott wrote that the new School of Home Economics would "suit the needs of the young women and will place the work in home economics on the same basis as that of engineering and agriculture."

The Home Economics Club for students was organized at Purdue in 1916. Once the department became a separate school, the club reorganized and changed its name to honor Virginia Meredith. It was then the Virginia C. Meredith Club. New members were voted into

The Home Economics Building opened in 1922 at the corner of West State and University Streets on the Purdue University campus. In this winter photograph, Model Ts park next to the building. The red brick structure was renamed Matthews Hall in 1976. Courtesy of Purdue University Libraries, Archives and Special Collections.

the club based on their grade point average. Virginia spoke at many meetings during the early years.

Mary Matthews was a charter member of the Delta Chapter of Omicron Nu, a home economics honor society that was installed in 1913. Omicron Nu emphasized scholarship, leadership, and research, but there was no research occurring in the department when the honor society began. Also in the early years, there were no student loan programs or emergency funds available. Mary kept a small personal emergency fund and quietly helped students when necessary. Her personal "scholarship program" was not common knowledge and reflected her discreet concern and support of students.

The goal of the School of Home Economics was to give the student training that would help her become a responsible citizen and an intelligent homemaker, plus prepare her with an occupation in order to be self-supporting. Mary was a forward thinker when it came to the roles of husbands and wives in the household. She was an early protagonist for what we now know as women's rights. She wrote in one of her textbooks, "In families where the housekeeper does the housework herself, this unpaid labor of hers is always equal in money value to the income contributed by those employed outside the home, a fact often not taken into consideration. The husband and wife should therefore consider the maintaining of a home as a partnership business which each should share equally." She also had opinions about how a couple should handle their finances. "When the man and woman marry, they assume that they can trust each other, yet after marriage many a husband assumes that he cannot trust his wife's judgment in money matters," she wrote. "The intelligent woman should be given joint management of the account."

Just before the establishment of the School of Home Economics, Mary had encouraged Laura Partch to form the Purdue University Nursery School to give students real practice in child care and management. Partch was a graduate of the Indianapolis City Hospital School of Nursing who taught classes in home nursing and child care. Perhaps the Nursery School was Mary's humane answer to the "practice baby" concept that was common among Practice Houses at other universities (see chapter 8.). The Nursery School was established in 1926 and was the first in Indiana. It was also the first of ten university-based nursery schools in the United States.

The nursery school was originally housed in the basement of "Building Two," so named because it was the second building on campus. It was a small structure located next to the Home Economics Building, where Beering Hall stands today. Sixteen children attended the first classes. Partch became the first director of the Purdue University Nursery School. A well-known early childhood educator, Katherine Haskill Read, taught at the nursery school. She received an MS from Purdue and then served as a Purdue college instructor. Read influenced the field of early childhood education worldwide for more than a half a century. She believed that self-understanding among teachers was critical in helping children understand themselves. Her "Guides to Speech and Action" have endured, and most are as relevant today as they were fifty years ago (e.g., "State suggestions or directions in a positive rather than negative form" and "Give the child a choice only when you intend to leave the choice up to him"). In 1950, Read wrote the first textbook for college students preparing to teach young children, *The Nursery School: A Human Relationships Laboratory*. The ninth edition of this book was published in 1993, and it has been printed in seven different languages. Read died in 1991.

In 1930, the American Home Economics Association reorganized to establish nine official professional departments, two of which were "family relations" and "child development." During this decade, Mary Matthews continued to increase emphasis on child care in her school. She established a playground east of the Home Economics Building where the Loeb Fountain flows today. Apple trees shaded the play area and a train track ran where the sidewalk is presently. Trains ran along this track to transport coal from the south end of campus to the power and heating plant near the Engineering Administration Building on the north side. This was where the landmark smokestacks once rose into the air.

Amelia Earhart and two students, Gabrielle Miles and Edna Hutson, observe children at the playground of the Purdue University Nursery School around 1935. Mary L. Matthews created Indiana's first nursery school in 1926 the same year she became Purdue's first dean of the School of Home Economics. Courtesy of Purdue University Libraries, Archives and Special Collections.

Professor Emeritus Mary Louise Foster remembers the Purdue University Nursery School when she was on staff with the child development program in the 1940s. "The problem was to get the children in to the playground before the train would come, one way or the other," she recalls. "The train engineer would honk the horn and wave at the kids on the playground. He would stop and talk to them, and he got to know their names. It was a fun time to be working with the child development program."

The trolley ran on the other side of the Home Economics Building on University Street. Between the screech and clang of the trolley and the grinding and tooting of the train, the area was very noisy. Foster said, "When the trolley went by and the windows were down because it was warm out, teachers had to stop talking and wait for the trolley to pass, so they could be heard."

A 1932 bulletin produced by the United States Department of the Interior states, "During the decade 1920-1930, the number of nursery schools reported to the United States Office of Education increased from 3 to 262. This last number does not comprise the total number of nursery schools in the United States, but the increase from 3 to 262 in the number reported indicates their rapid growth." The bulletin, with a cover image of a curly-haired boy in knickers, further explains that with families moving to cities and having fewer children, there is a need for a "substitute" to offer "the wholesome give and take which living with other children affords." It states, "The excitements of city life are over stimulating for young children." Some of the bulletin's content could be written today, for the basic goals of parenting have not changed. The piece continues, "Women are seeking employment outside the home both to add to the family income and to carry on vocations or avocations. Parents want the best environment for their children and are seeking guidance in their profession of parenthood."

Parents were as eager for knowledge then as now. Mary understood their interest. At that time, a series of Parent's Institutes were offered on campus that drew as many as four hundred people to a session.

In 1932, Mary was named Indiana Federation of Clubs chairman of the Department of Education, a post she held for twenty years. Mary was an advocate for parents and teachers, and for thirty years she served the Indiana Congress of Parents and Teachers. She was the chairman of Home and Family Life, which represented the key area of all parent-teacher development. During a PTA Founders Day dinner in 1952, the year Mary retired, Allan A. Smith said, "We can never repay Dean Mary for her many services, but we will always remember her selfless devotion to the cause of child welfare."

Eventually, there were two nursery schools equipped to care for thirty children at Purdue University. Graduate assistants in the Department of Foods and Nutrition served as nursery school dietitians. Interestingly, that department also offered a 1933 course in foods for men "who were doing their own cooking." Marion Mattson, who had a PhD from the University of Minnesota's Institute of Child Welfare, became director of the Purdue University Nursery School and an assistant professor of home administration. During World War II, she was a member of the Indiana State Committee on Care of Children in Wartime, which worked with the Indiana State Defense Council and the Indiana State Nutrition Council to prepare a guide entitled *Feeding Children in Group Care.* The light blue cover of the guide depicts a hand drawing of a mother feeding her three children at the dinner table, framed by an outline of the state of Indiana. The typed guide reads, "While mothers work in our war plants, their children must be afforded the same care and consideration they would have under a normal home atmosphere. . . . As a guide for the many workers who are now concerned with the care of children in the newly established day care centers for children of working mothers, this booklet has been prepared by a committee of the Indiana State Nutrition Council at the request of the Indiana State Committee on Care of Children in Wartime." Two other Purdue faculty members were on the committee: Assistant Professor of Foods and Nutrition Cecelia Schuck and Associate Professor Institution Management Ruby Clark. The back of the guide depicts a drawing of a family encircled with the words, "U.S. needs us strong. Eat the basic 7 every day." This was part of a push to encourage people to eat foods from what was then deemed the basic seven food groups:

1. green and yellow vegetables

2. oranges, tomatoes, grapefruit

3. potatoes and other vegetables and fruits

4. milk and milk products

5. meat, poultry, fish, or eggs

6. bread, flour, and cereals

7. butter and fortified margarine

Some of the early Purdue home economics staff members included Edith Gamble, who was an assistant in household economics, and Amy L Howe, who was head of clothing and textiles. Gamble and Howe were very good friends. Dorothy Marquis Culver, a 1930 graduate, said, "Amy Howe—I was scared to death of at first. She was very formal, but I got to know her, and she was a wonderful person. She helped a lot of girls through school. I was in school during the depression and the banks had closed."

Gertrude Sunderlin came to Purdue in 1931 and headed up experimental foods. She was the first woman to earn a PhD from Iowa State's College of Home Economics. Margaret Beeman arrived at Purdue in 1935 to be the assistant to Dean Mary Matthews. The dietetics program at Purdue was the first in Indiana. Amy Bloye headed the department. She had been an instructor before home economics moved from the School of Science. Lella and Kate Gaddis were friends with Bloye. Kate writes in her 1933 diary, "Went down to Amy Bloye's for supper. She has such a nice apartment. Had a fine time."

Ardath Unrau Johnson came to work in the Department of Foods and Nutrition as a graduate assistant in 1936. She said, "We respected our superiors. The thing I remember about Dean Matthews was that she made me feel very welcome. Because I was kind of a greenhorn from the farm. I was a country gal. She had a way of making me feel like I was important."

In the early years, all of the home economics majors and classes were in one building, so all of the students and teachers saw each other frequently and were close. Often, when a new staff member arrived by train, Mary Matthews or members of her department would personally pick up the woman at the downtown Lafayette Big Four Depot and take her to lunch or dinner. Home economics women took care of their own. Similarly, Lella Gaddis was close to the men of the School of Agriculture, sharing many meals with them and their families over the years, including holidays and birthdays. For both Mary and Lella, the people with whom they worked were like an extended family.

Alice Nickel Chitty remembered a special lab: "[Miss White] was in charge of the rat lab. We fed rats all of the different kinds of diets, and [recorded] the results. I happen to live just across the street from the home economics building. So, that made it real easy to feed my rats. I had to feed the rats of my roommates when they were gone."

Janet Orem Parvis came to Purdue to get her home economics degree in 1930. She said, "They turned me over to Miss Gamble. There never was one more near an angel; I'm sure on this earth. She took me under her wing. She shepherded me through. I don't know what I would have done without her." After Parvis graduated and was hired as a staff member, she got to know Edith Gamble on a professional level as well. Years later, Gamble needed her friends. Parvis said, "When Miss Gamble was in a nursing home, she needed to be fed, so we [Home Economics staff] took turns going to feed her. On football game days, the people who usually fed her couldn't make it there through the traffic, so I always fed her on Saturday night. I hope I repaid a little bit what she did for me."

Opal Stech graduated from Purdue in 1932. She taught home economics at all levels and worked as an extension specialist. Stech said of Mary Matthews: "She followed up on all of her students. Even after we graduated and came back as alumni, she would always say, 'Now, what have you been doing?' She wanted to know the contributions we were making."

Obtaining necessary tools and equipment was sometimes difficult for the School of Home Economics. Mary Edith Frist Banes, a kindergarten teacher in Lafayette for thirty-three years, came to Purdue at age seventeen in 1938. Banes took a sewing class from Amy Howe. Banes said, "I could not do my project till I had a pair of left-handed scissors, because I was left-handed. So I waited six weeks to start my project."

Esther Hohlt Sohl graduated from the School of Home Economics in 1934. She said, "I remember Miss Matthews. I was always a little in awe. She had such dignity and when she talked to us, we listened."

In 1939, Purdue finally recognized that women might want an optional curriculum that was not in the realm of homemaking and began to offer more "scientific" options. Mary created a course for men and women entitled "Some Problems in Right Living." In the book she authored, *Elementary Home Economics*, Mary wrote a section titled "To the Student," which reads in part:

> Right living begins with the home. Who makes the home? The man may furnish the money to build and maintain the

house, but it is the woman who plans and manages the home. It is her business to see that the family lives in a sanitary and an attractive house; that every member of the family has clean, properly selected and well cooked food; that everyone is suitably clothed; that the family income is wisely spent, and that all in the home are helped to lead a happy and useful life.

The same year the School of Home Economics was established at Purdue, the American Home Economics Association (now the American Association of Family and Consumer Sciences, AAFCS) sponsored a national design contest among leading art schools to adopt a symbol that embodied the home, household arts, and their scientific application in the home. There were sixty submissions. Mildred Chamberlain of Chicago won the contest with her logo design depicting the Betty Lamp. She said, "The lamp in colonial days had provided light for all household industries."

The Betty Lamp evolved from simple clay dish lamps that were used as long ago as 6,000 BC. As time passed, these dish-like lamps were made of iron, copper, and bronze. They burned fish oil or scraps of fat and had wicks of twisted cloth. These early lamps were improved by creating a wick holder in the base, which channeled the drippings from the wick back into the bowl of the lamp. The curved handle had a short chain attached with a hook on one end for hanging the lamp and a pick on the other for rescuing the wick from the oil. This "better" lamp, named Betty, from the German words "*besser*" or "*bete*," meaning "to make better," produced comparatively good light for its time and was used widely by early American colonists. Representing the light in the home and the light of the mind, the Betty Lamp was a good choice as the symbol of home economics. The winning design was announced in the December 1927 issue of the *Journal of Home Economics*. The School of Home Economics at Purdue incorporated a Betty Lamp into its logo after the symbol was adopted.

The Betty Lamp is still the icon of the AAFCS and is used in many ways as a symbol in schools of consumer and family sciences at universities around the country. From a California State University student newsletter named "The Betty" to lighting a lamp at consumer and family sciences ceremonies, the Betty Lamp continues to illuminate the connection between home and family arts and sciences to the students of schools of higher learning. The Web site of the Pennsylvania Association of Family and Consumer Sciences, Inc., an affiliate of the American Association of Family and Consumer Sciences, Inc., reads, "The beam of the Betty Lamp symbolizes: need of exact knowledge; appreciation of beauty; spirit of joy; power of strength; blessing of fellowship; satisfaction of achievement; value of service; and bond of cooperation."

Virginia Meredith was eighty-five when the Chicago World's Fair: A Century of Progress Exposition of 1933 took place. During "Chicago Week" at the fair, officials paid tribute to those living and dead who produced the "White City" forty years before during the World's Columbian Exposition. Mary Matthews accompanied her mother to the fair, along with Maurice Murphy, an Indianapolis newspaperwoman. Officials honored Virginia as one of the few surviving members of the famous Board of Lady Managers of the 1893 exposition. Only a handful of members of Bertha Palmer's board were still living, and Virginia was the only one to visit A Century of Progress. An exposition automobile was sent to Virginia's hotel to chauffeur the three women to the fair.

Virginia was very interested in seeing the sights, but Mary kept a watchful eye over her mother to prevent her from attempting to cover the entire exposition during her two-day visit. Rufus C. Dawes, president of the fair, received Virginia in the administration building. Virginia told Dawes, "I came to Chicago feeling that I would see an interesting and different world's fair, but not one comparable with that of 1893. But I was greatly surprised. This fair is so different in architecture and color, and it also is a greater fair. More marvelous is the fact that it produced and opened in these times of economic stress." Virginia was referring to the Great Depression the country was experiencing at the time.

Lella and Kate Gaddis made three separate trips to see the sights at the Chicago World's Fair. Kate wrote, "The Century of Progress is wonderful. So many interesting things and such vivid coloring. Miles to walk. Saw Wings of a Century." "Wings of a Century" was an elaborate outdoor pageant along the shoreline of Lake Michigan that told the double story of the progress in transportation running side by side with "America's hundred-year march from a small pioneer nation to a leader in world affairs." The pageant was enacted on a huge triple stage. There were one hundred fifty performers, ten trains, early automobiles, boats, and a model of the Wright brothers' plane. The final scene was a "trip to Mars."

Virginia Meredith insisted on seeing the Indiana exhibit even though it had stirred much controversy. Artist Thomas Hart Benton had been commissioned to paint a mural for the Indiana Hall. Benton's work stood out for its scale and artistic impact, and for him it was "a dream fulfilled." It was a continuous mural, twelve feet high and about two hundred fifty feet long. For inspiration, Benton traveled Indiana with an eye to capture not just the grand sweep of its history, but also the homey details that were the backdrop of that history. The mural depicted the social, economic, and cultural history of the Hoosier state and landed him on the cover of *Time* magazine in 1934. Yet Benton's mural sparked controversy even before it was completed. One of his drawings, then as now, ignited hot disagreement. What is now known as Cultural Panel 10, "Parks, the Circus, the Klan, the Press," led some to proclaim Benton's piece as "vulgar" for a painting that they believed should have shown Indiana citizens in the very best light. Cultural Panel 10 depicted the Ku Klux Klan, an undeniable reality of the previous decade. Yet even though there were critics, others believed that the mural made Indiana's exhibit the most artistic at the exposition. After the fair, the mural panels were placed in storage in a horse barn at the state fairgrounds in Indianapolis. They languished there until 1937, when the president of Indiana University, Herman B. Wells, obtained the paintings for the price of shipping. He placed most of the panels in the IU Auditorium.

After Virginia Meredith toured the Indiana exhibit at the fair and viewed Benton's bold work, she declared, "Perhaps strangely, I like it very much."

In the last years of Virginia's life, she would cross paths with famous aviatrix Amelia Earhart, whom President Elliott hired in 1935. For about six weeks each year until her fateful flight in 1937, Earhart lived on campus and worked with women students as a career advisor. She gave lectures on opportunities for women and on aviation. In 1934, Virginia introduced Earhart before she spoke to about five hundred members of the University Club. Lella and Kate Gaddis were in the audience (Kate wrote that she wore her new blue dress), and more than likely, Mary Matthews was in attendance. Virginia provided opening remarks when Earhart spoke again the following year to nearly 3,500 when she was formally presented as a faculty member. Virginia described Earhart as courageous in her work and that she broke down the "competitive struggle for social advantage between men and women." Earhart herself said, "Often youngsters are sadly miscast. I have known girls who should be tinkering with mechanical things instead of making dresses, and boys who would be better at cooking than engineering" (*Last Flight*, 1937). Lella and Kate had just moved into a new house that week. Kate records in her diary on November 12, 1935, "We had our first meal in the new house last night. We did not go to hear Amelia Earhart Putnam. Too tired."

The Past State Presidents of Indiana Extension Homemakers Association was organized on January 15, 1936, during a breakfast in the Peasant Room of the Purdue Memorial Union building. Lella Gaddis attended. One of the purposes of the organization that consisted of all the past presidents (seventy-one at the time) was to promote the Indiana Home Economics Association Loan Fund, named the Virginia C. Meredith Student Loan Fund in 1941. The Past State Presidents were proud to have had the opportunity to serve IEHA and wanted a special group to show their gratitude for the top leadership role. Their annual meetings were held during the Agricultural Conference. A plaque with the presidents' names hangs today in the John Purdue Room, located in Stone Hall. Later a contest was held to design a Past State Presidents pin, which was given to all members. The first breakfast was a lovely affair, and a description of the table setting was included in the minutes: "The centerpiece consisted of a silver bowl with white poinsettias with white tapers on each side set in silver candlesticks with a white poinsettia base. The corsages were made of silver cloth and silver leaves. The place cards were white with the names printed in silver." The group voted to send Virginia Meredith a note telling her of the creation and goals of the Past State Presidents' organization.

Virginia made her last public speech on May 19, 1936, at a School of Home Economics tenth anniversary dinner honoring Mary Mathews. She and her daughter had accomplished so much for Purdue and for women. At the honorary table with Virginia and Mary were, among others, David Ross and Dean Dorothy C. Stratton. Kate Gaddis made mention of the event in her dairy: "Had a big party for Miss Matthews." Soon after that proud day, Virginia suffered a heart attack that left her bedridden. Her fellow trustees sent her roses and a get-well note, but Virginia would never again attend a meeting. She passed away on December 10 in the home she shared with Mary on Waldron Street. She was eighty-eight years old.

Kate recorded the news in her diary that day, writing, "Mrs. Meredith died at 4:30." The following day she wrote, "Lella out scouting for a Purdue Trustee?" Virginia's position as a trustee was vacant. Was

Virginia Meredith made her last public speech at the dinner celebrating the tenth anniversary of the School of Home Economics at Purdue University on May 19, 1936. Pictured are Margaret Beeman (head of home economics at Ball State University), Mrs. Edward Elliott, David Ross, Virginia Meredith, Mrs. R. D. Canan, Dean Mary L. Matthews, and Dean Dorothy Stratton. Courtesy of Purdue University Libraries, Archives and Special Collections.

Lella helping her friend and Purdue University Trustee David Ross consider possible replacements?

Newspapers from around the country announced Virginia's death. Honoring her request, a simple service was held at her home. The School of Home Economics cancelled classes that morning to allow students and faculty to attend. At 9:30, buglers at various stations on campus played "Taps" and all activities stopped. The American flag flew at half-mast. Pallbearers included President Edward Elliott and Dean A. A. Potter. The Lafayette *Journal and Courier* noted the funeral "was free of all ostentation, its simplicity reflecting the gentle nature of the woman who had earned a state's gratitude for outstanding civic service."

After the service, many in attendance traveled to Cambridge City, Indiana. As they passed through Indianapolis, the funeral procession was provided with a police escort. Virginia was buried next to her husband, Henry, in the Riverside Cemetery in Cambridge City. Virginia had completed her will nearly ten years before her death. It was a brief, handwritten half-page note that said:

> On this second day of May 1927–I, Virginia C. Meredith, do make this my last will–I give and bequeath to Mary Lockwood Matthews my household goods, furniture and silver– Also give and bequeath to her any and all property of any description that I may have at the time of my death–I do this in recognition of the affection and care which she has given to me, and trusting her to give to Meredith Matthews, to Virginia C. Miller (niece) and Austin B. Claypool (nephew) some suitable memento or remembrance of me.

The following January, Purdue University paid homage to Virginia with a memorial held at Eliza Fowler Hall, fittingly, during the annual Agricultural Conference and Farm Bureau Day.

When Virginia died, Purdue lost a warrior for women, agriculture, home economics, and the University as a whole. Mary lost a mother.

On the Air

In the late 1920s, Kate and Lella had their first experience with a radio in their home. They walked across the street and listened to the radio of their tenants, Assistant Director of Agricultural Extension Tom Coleman and his family. Then they began "trying out" various models. Kate records:

> December 12, 1928: Woolevers bring a Majestic Radio over. Too much noise for us, I am afraid.

> December 13: The Reeds down for supper. Hard to tell which wants to fuss most with the radio—father or son. [Harry Reed and family rented an apartment in the Gaddis home. Later, he was dean of the School of Agriculture.]

> December 19: I am having such a good time radioing.

> January 5, 1929: We are enjoying the radio so much. One gets the news at home.

> January 10: We are trying out a Brownie Radio. Like it very much.

> February 1: Have an Ozarka radio on trial. Too noisy.

February 11: We have an Atwater Kent radio and like it very much. Having tried out many.

February 19: Pay $180.25 for the radio tonight.

March 4: Herbert Hoover becomes President of the U.S. Calvin Coolidge retires. Lella hears it over the radio.

Lella and Kate not only owned a radio, they also broadcasted on the radio. The "Purdue Threshing Ring" program was a night program on Chicago radio station WLS, which was owned by *Prairie Farmer* magazine, an affiliate of Farm Progress. The station was known as "WLS, The Prairie Farmer Station" and beheld the legendary "Cornstalk Studio." It was famous for its radio artists like Gene Autry, Little Georgie Gobel, and Lulu Belle, plus the Saturday night WLS National Barn Dance that was broadcast live from the Eighth Street Theater. From 1928 to 1960, WLS featured programming for the farm families of the Midwest. It was one of the country's greatest radio stations. On several occasions, Lella drove to Chicago to broadcast on the "Purdue Threshing Ring" program. The sound of a threshing machine began every show, which offered agricultural information from Purdue staff and faculty. Radio was the latest, most sophisticated way Agricultural Extension could reach thousands of farm families with one "demonstration." Local county associations and Home Economics Clubs were encouraged to hold their meetings and feature the program. This Purdue relationship with WLS continued throughout the 1930s. Later, the program moved to WOWO, Fort Wayne; WFBM, Indianapolis; and WHAS, Louisville.

Lella and her Agricultural Extension allies gathered around the carbon microphone and told Midwest farm families about the latest developments in farming and home arts. Kate Gaddis sat at home in West Lafayette with an ear to her Atwater Kent, adjusting the dial to lessen the static and hear her sister's voice across the airwaves.

Teachers and children from Lafayette schools broadcasted on local radio, and Kate had her turn. She notes on May 14, 1937, "This is the day I do the broadcasting. Not such a bad thing. I talked on birds. They said it was ok."

Lella Gaddis (right) visits with Gladys Blair on January 3, 1947 at a tea held the year Lella retired as state leader of home demonstration agents at Purdue University. Blair was the home and household editor for The Prairie Press *and edited* Prairie Farmer—WLS Cookbook, Centennial Edition *published in 1941.* Courtesy of Purdue University Libraries, Archives and Special Collections.

In the next decade, the Great Depression hit and people listened to the radio to uplift them during the major economic crisis. President Roosevelt was the first "radio president" and his "fireside chats" helped give confidence to Americans during their darkest hours.

The 1920s ended with the Gaddis sisters' good friends George Christie, director of Agricultural Extension, and his wife moving to Canada. At school, Kate's students were raising money to buy an elephant for the Columbian Park Zoo. The main animal house was constructed in 1928, and it remains today. Kate saw the fundraising as an inconvenience. She writes:

> January 31, 1929: The dads and the Optimists Club play basketball for money for the elephant. This blamed elephant.

> February 12: Went to a card party to help pay for the elephant. Centennial [school] giving the party. Lincoln [school] gets to name it. "Linco."

Columbian Park Zoo, which dates back to 1908, is one of the oldest zoos in Indiana. One of the first animals was "Linco" the elephant, who was purchased from the Hagenbeck-Wallace Circus in Peru, Indiana. Nearly ten thousand students in Lafayette and West Lafayette raised more than $2,000 toward the purchase of the elephant, then named "Ruth." Lincoln School was the only school for black elementary and middle school children from the late 1880s until 1951, when it was integrated. Most likely, the Lincoln School students were the poorest of the community, yet they exceeded their school's fundraising goal and earned the honor of renaming the elephant Linco.

Over the course of Kate's late 1920s and early 1930s diaries, she notes that Lella continued to see "Friend Dave" regularly for dinner and weekend stays with Kate as chaperone. A couple of Kate's entries refer to David Ross as "The Trustee." Lella attended a party David Ross hosted to benefit Lafayette Home Hospital. The sisters also toured a new apartment building close to campus, "The Varsity," which Kate described as "lovely." The Varsity Apartments still stand today across from Harry's Chocolate Shop. The sisters bought a new GE icebox for $282.50, and Kate noted, "That includes box." Kate wrote about famed aviator Charles Lindbergh in April 1930, saying, "Lindbergh flew across the U.S. in 14 hours and 7 minutes." Notes about Lindbergh continue to appear:

> June 22, 1930: Lindberghs have baby boy.

> March 1, 1932: Lindbergh baby kidnapped tonight.

> March 2: No word of Lindbergh baby

> March 18: No word of the Lindbergh baby

> April 4: They have not found the Lindbergh baby yet, but are hopeful.

May 12: The Lindbergh baby found in bushes 4 miles from home. Head crushed. Went to church supper. Lella Altrusa.

May 13: Lindy identifies the baby by its hair, teeth and toes. They have it cremated.

Charles and Anne Morrow Lindbergh's infant son was kidnapped, and a $50,000 ransom was paid, but the baby was found dead. The case was considered the crime of the century. The nation's concern and horror resulted in laws that expanded the role of federal law enforcement agencies in dealing with such crimes, including allowing the government to demand the death penalty for kidnappers who take victims across state lines. Kate notes the conclusion of the sad affair on April 3, 1936: "Bruno Hauptmann was electrocuted for the murder of the Lindbergh baby. The case cost $2,000,000, which occurred four years ago."

Kate's journals reflect the country's climate during the Great Depression. In the fall of 1931 she wrote, "The Depression seems greater. Wheat and corn, per bushel, 25 cents. Oats, 12 cents. Abundance of peaches and apples. All vegetables cheap." She wrote of the Farmers and Traders Bank and Rossville bank closing, describing the time as "a dreadful spell of Depression." Yet the following January when the annual Agriculture Conference was held at Purdue, there was record attendance in spite of the country's economic devastation. Franklin Roosevelt was elected in 1932, and Kate wrote at the end of the year, "The Depression still on worse than ever. The Democrats will have full savvy. They say 'Things will be better.' Rents and salaries reduced, but glad we have them." Before Roosevelt takes office, he has a brush with death, which Kate records.

February 15, 1933: Some crazy foreigner tries to kill President-elect Roosevelt. Wounded the Mayor of Chicago. Happened at Miami, Florida.

March 4: Roosevelt was inaugurated the 32 president of the U.S. amid much rejoicing. Happy Days are here again. Let us hope so.

> March 6: Mayor Cermak of Chicago died last night from
> the shot fired by Zangara meant for the President-elect Roo-
> sevelt.

> March 7: Banks all over U.S. closed yesterday. Congress to
> take care of us. Fortunately, I have some money to tide us
> over until things settle.

American citizen Giuseppe Zangara, originally from Italy, fired five
shots at Roosevelt. Four people were wounded and Chicago Mayor An-
ton Cermak was killed. Zangara was found guilty of murder and was
executed on March 20, 1933.

Roosevelt introduced the "New Deal" to transform America's economy, which had been shattered by the Wall Street crash. Roosevelt's first act as president was to confront the country's banking
crisis. Since the beginning of the Great Depression, many banks had
been forced to close. As a consequence, many people lost their life's
savings. By the beginning of 1933, the American people were losing
faith in their banking system and some withdrew their money and
kept it at home. The day after taking office as president, Roosevelt
ordered all banks to close. He then asked Congress to pass legislation
that would guarantee that those with savings would not lose their
money if there were to be another financial crisis.

In Roosevelt's first one hundred days, many acts were introduced
that were to form the basis of the New Deal. On March 20, Roosevelt
asked Congress to pass the Beer Act, which was one of the actions that
eventually ended Prohibition. Beer sales would raise revenue for the
government through taxes, and the Beer Act would also introduce a
morale booster in that people would no longer be criminalized because they wanted a drink. Kate was not pleased. The week before
Easter Sunday, she notes:

> March 22: The President signs Beer Bill. The world seems
> crazy of the idea of beer. I am ashamed.

> April 6: All talk now is beer goes into effect at midnight.
> Too bad.

April 7: Beer back again. Many, many seem happy, and the amber fluid flows freely. Such a shame.

April 8: We go over to town and never saw so many people in the streets.

Some of Roosevelt's New Deal programs became the responsibility of the Agricultural Extension agent. Lella and her staff encouraged the cultivation of "subsistence gardens" in rural and urban areas, and the teaching of gardening skills. Once again, the home demonstration agent emphasized the conservation and preservation of food. New Deal emergency money helped keep extension alive and growing.

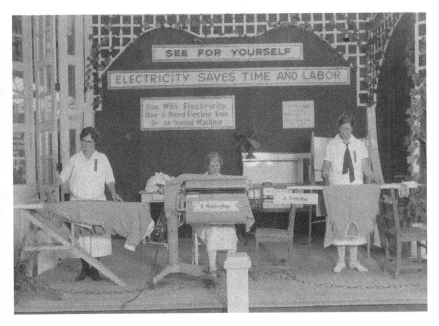

Lella Gaddis (center) and two of her county agents demonstrate how electricity can save time and labor when ironing at this Household Electrical Exhibit in the Purdue Building at the Indiana State Fair in 1933. During this time, Lella and her staff were vital in helping Indiana women and their families endure the Great Depression. Courtesy of Purdue University Libraries, Archives and Special Collections.

Kate mentioned the various plays, movies, and concerts that she and Lella attended. In 1933, she saw *The Wizard of Oz*. This was a local play, for the famous movie would not be produced until 1939. The next year, while Lella was gone on one of her many overnight stays, Kate saw the black and white "talkie" *Wonder Bar*, of which she wrote, "Why do people be such fools?" *Wonder Bar* starred Al Jolson and was about murder and romance in a Parisian nightclub. Interestingly, Louise Fazenda, one of the actresses in the movie, was born in Lafayette, Indiana. Also that year, Kate saw Will Rogers in *Handy Andy*. She wrote, "Why can't they have more nice, clean shows?" On October 9, 1934, Kate notes, "Went to see Mae West last night. Never again."

❧

In 1935, Lella and Kate built their final home on property they purchased from Harry J. Reed, their long-time friend and downstairs tenant who would become dean of the School of Agriculture. Kate records the details:

> January 26: Pay H.J. $1500 for the lot on Grant Street.

> June 29: Looks like the new house is a go. Lella signed on the dotted line for $9491. Will get a government loan for $7500 for ten years.

The remainder of the year, Kate wrote of the construction of their house at 1004 North Grant Street, across the street from West Lafayette High School. In the middle of the summer, Kate noted that the sisters' brother, Clyde, was sick, and she cashed a $50 savings bond to help with his bills. Lella and Kate made a trip to Indianapolis and purchased light fixtures, a rug for the hall, and draperies. The home would have a dumbwaiter, a miniature elevator used to transport food and more from the main floor down to the basement. Often Lella and Kate would use the dumbwaiter when they hosted children's birthday parties in the basement, moving cake and ice cream to the lower floor. They had parties for the children of their neighbors and friends. In September, the sisters received a telegram saying that Clyde had died. The next day, Kate boarded her first air-conditioned train and headed to Cushing, Oklahoma for her brother's funeral. Lella did not go, probably because of work commitments.

The house was to be finished by November 1. That day, Lella returned from a conference in Washington, DC and found the house not completed as promised. The sisters had already rented out their current living quarters on Russell Street. Lella was not pleased, and she let the builder know her feelings. Kate said there was "much fussing around," And on November 3 she notes, "We are sleeping at the Reeds. Seems funny not to have a place to lay your head, of your own."

On a rainy day in the middle of the month, the women moved into their lovely new home, the last in which they would reside.

On April 14, Wiley Post, the first pilot to fly solo around the world, landed his "Winnie Mae" at the Purdue Airport, and Lella and Kate were there to see him. Post had attempted four high altitude transcontinental flights that year, all of which failed. The third inadvertently ended at Purdue. His plane developed trouble, and he was forced to land after circling the airport several times. Word spread around the community, and people came running to see, having no idea a famous aviator was overhead until Post landed and stepped out of his plane wearing his signature white eye patch. Lella and Kate saw the famed aviator on one of his last flights. Kate notes on July 16, "Will Rogers and Wiley Post killed last night in a plane in Alaska. Taken to a Presbyterian hospital."

Will Rogers had asked Post to fly him through Alaska in search of new material for his newspaper column. Post and Rogers left Seattle in early August and made several stops in Alaska. While Post piloted the aircraft, Rogers wrote his columns on his typewriter. On takeoff from a lagoon near Point Barrow, the engine failed, and the aircraft plunged into the water. Both men died instantly.

At that time in 1935, Kate was suffering with stiff and sore knees and feet. Once school was over in June, Lella took her to Battle Creek Sanitarium in Battle Creek, Michigan. Battle Creek Sanitarium was like a posh resort and holistic health spa as well as a hospital. Kate said it was a beautiful place, and her room cost $1.50 per day. Kate received a teacher's discount for her stay. Famous surgeon John Harvey Kellogg, who had been the young star of the Seventh-Day Adventist

Church's health mission, was the superintendent there. Kellogg was a leading advocate of the vegetarian diet. He and his wife, Ella, invented food products to help patients stay well once they returned to their homes. One of the nutrition experts who worked for Kellogg was Lenna Cooper, who was later a contributing founder of the American Dietetic Association. Later the doctor's brother, Will Kellogg, saw the commercial potential of the food products and built the business that is today a household name. The guests of the opulent Battle Creek Sanitarium included those at the top of society's hierarchy, such as C. W. Barron, Henry Ford, S. Kresge, and Harvey Firestone. Kate writes of the experience:

> June 17: All days seem alike. You bathe, eat, see the doctor, then eat again. Teeth x-rayed. One bad one.
>
> June 18: Nothing unusual happens. You sit on the porch and talk to your newly made friends.
>
> June 19: Went to see the foot doctor. He thinks my shoes are all right. But need a little padding.
>
> June 22: Another day of the same. Not much time for anything but bathe, eat and sleep. Heard Dr. Kellogg.

Lella wrote letters to Kate while she was away. She told her about a raise she received that Kate said would help with their new car. At the end of the month, Lella arrived to take Kate home. Kate said, "It has been a restful two weeks. I hope my knees will be better."

The fall of 1936 brought events like attending a convocation to hear Amelia Earhart speak; seeing the best picture of the year, *The Great Ziegfeld*, starring William Powell, which Kate said was a lovely show; and Kate purchasing a fur coat. She writes of the splurge on November 27, "I went to Indianapolis. Get a new fur coat for $339.75. A lot to pay. They all seem to like it at the office."

Normally, Kate was very frugal, writing down in her diary her expenditures and marking each payday. Yet she also talked of shopping for new clothes, and she enjoyed fashion. Her purchase of an expensive fur coat was a bit out of character, but she had been through a lot with her health, and the next year she would be in her fiftieth year of teaching at age seventy. Perhaps she felt she deserved a beautiful garment that she could rightly afford. Though the Great Depression raged on, the Gaddis women were still faring well.

A couple of months later, Kate was sick again. She spent a month in the hospital. The women of the Purdue School of Home Economics gave her "a lovely box of paper and stamps." She received visitors and flowers, noting on February 25, 1937, "One finds how many friends you have when sick."

That year, Amelia Earhart prepared her Lockheed Electra "flying laboratory" at the Purdue Airport before her ill-fated world flight. She left Miami, Florida on June 1 and was lost on July 2 while attempting to land on Howland Island in the Pacific. Kate writes:

July 7: No word from Amelia Earhart since Friday.

September 21: Amelia Earhart has not been heard of for over a month. Went down as they think on her trip.

Kate kept her ear to current events, and she made a prophetic statement around that time: "War seems to be all we hear over the radio. I do hope we are not so foolish as to get mixed up in the affair."

On January 16, 1941, the Indiana Home Economics Association (IHEA) honored Lella Gaddis for twenty-five years of service as state leader of home demonstration with the unveiling of her portrait painted by Randolph Coats. During the annual Agricultural Conference, a special program took place in the Purdue Hall of Music, today Elliott Hall of Music. The Hall of Music had been completed the previous May. The program included Golda Brown, president of the IHEA, who presided over the grand affair. Organ music played, and Dean Mary Matthews spoke with a "Reminiscence." The Tippecanoe County Chorus performed under the direction of Al Stewart. Minnie Price, state leader of home demonstration at Ohio State University said a few words, and artist Randolph Coats was introduced. Coats was the perfect choice to paint a portrait of Lella. He was born in Richmond, Indiana, and he studied at what is now known as the Herron School of Art and Design in Indianapolis. Coats spent time painting in the Smoky Mountains and Indiana's Brown County. Lella frequented Brown County on her travels for extension and collected art from what was known as the Brown County Art Colony. Coats's favorite subjects were landscapes, but he was also well known for his portraits and figure painting. Coats painted or restored portraits of nearly forty Indiana governors.

The portrait of Lella Gaddis was unveiled on the massive Hall of Music stage and presented to Purdue University. Mrs. L. G. Clendenning, past president of the IHEA, said, "May this portrait always instill in the hearts of those who see it a desire to live up to her high ideals, and may we and our posterity never cease to be grateful for the great work she had done." President Edward Elliott accepted the portrait, and the gala event ended with organ music. The printed program for the event highlighted the growth of home economics demonstration under Lella's leadership. When she began work in 1914, there were seventy-five home economics organizations in the state with 3,131 women attending. In 1940, there were ninety-one participating counties out of ninety-two counties in the state with a membership of 40,059. The program said of Lella, "her great aim has been, along with the more practical side, to show them [women of Indiana] how to more fully appreciate the beauty of their homes in the open country and to enjoy the little things that go to make up daily living there."

As a further tribute that year, Lella was made honorary president of the IHEA, a position she held until 1960.

The portrait of Lella was displayed in the vast center stairwell of the Agriculture Administration Building alongside other portraits that lined the walls. Walking up the steps, visitors looked eye to eye with the great leaders (all men, except for Lella) of Purdue's School of Agriculture. Early on, Lella's portrait hung next to her two colleagues and longtime friends with whom she had worked countless hours and supped at innumerable dinners, birthday parties, and Christmas gatherings—John H. Skinner, dean of the School of Agriculture from 1907 to 1939, and his successor as dean, Harry J. Reed, who was also the director of the Agricultural Experimental Station. Lella had cared for their children, been Reed's landlord, and purchased land owned by Reed on which she built her home on Grant Street. These three comrades ignited the early days of Purdue's land-grant mission. It was

The Indiana Home Economics Association honored Lella Reed Gaddis for 25 years of service as state leader of home demonstration agents with the presentation of her portrait painted by Randolph Coats to Purdue University in 1941. The painting was missing for several years before it was discovered in disrepair and then refurbished. Today, the portrait is located in Matthews Hall. Courtesy of Purdue University Libraries, Archives and Special Collections.

natural that Lella's portrait would hang next to those of Skinner and Reed.

However, later, Lella's portrait vanished.

Many years passed, and Lella's family noticed that the portrait was no longer on display in the Agriculture Administration Building. Lella's great-niece, Miriam Epple-Heath, had an opportunity to express her feelings about the missing portrait to a Purdue staff member. She said, "I'll tell you something that really hurts me. My first husband's great-aunt Lella Gaddis had a portrait done by Randolph Coats, and it has somehow disappeared. It used to hang in Ag Hall. My sister-in-law, a relative of Lella Gaddis, asked several years ago where it was. They said they had put it upstairs, which equated to the attic. They replaced it with Earl Butz. My sister-in-law said, 'It's strange to me how you could have someone who had an admirable departure as well as an admirable career at Purdue, displaced by someone who was imprisoned.'" Epple-Heath's sister-in-law was referring to an incident in 1981 when Earl Butz pleaded guilty to federal tax evasion charges for having underreported income he had earned in 1978. He was sentenced to five years in prison, however, all but thirty days of the term was suspended. Eventually, with Epple-Heath's persuasion, Lella's portrait was located in the attic of the Agriculture Administration Building. The painting had been scuffed and the frame was in pieces. The painting was restored and hung in Matthews Hall where it remains today, a single portrait in the first floor hallway.

War Stories

After the Japanese attacked Pearl Harbor on December 7, 1941, the United States declared war on Japan and Germany. Once America became involved in World War II, Purdue's School of Home Economics expanded its course offerings to include "wartime cookery" and "canteen classes." Dean Mary Matthews served as director of home economics for the Indiana Food Administration and was a member of the Indiana State Council of Defense. During this time of rationing, blackouts, and fire drills, the Indiana State Council of Defense was established to coordinate civil defense, boost war production in Hoosier factories, and raise money for the war effort through bond drives. Mary worked in the thick of those efforts. The men and some women went off to war, and the Purdue campus was sparsely populated.

Alice Ford Wright, a 1936 home economics graduate, said, "I particularly remember Dean Matthews. During World War II, Everett [Wright's husband] was sent to the South Pacific. One day I went up to Purdue just to knock around and see who all I knew. Dean Matthews was one of them. She said, 'What are you going to do?' I said, 'I don't know what I'm going to do.' She said, 'Well, I do. You're going to come in and be in Home Management #1. You have to teach the laundry class.' So, I was on the staff at Purdue. I taught laundry. But

Dean Matthews was really my lifesaver, because as far as I was concerned, the world had practically come to an end."

The war created considerable demand for technically trained personnel. Anna Akeley came to campus in 1942 as a bride of Edward Akeley, a theoretical physicist at Purdue. Anna, who was from Vienna, Austria, had escaped from Nazi Germany, fleeing through Russia and Siberia. In Europe, Anna had studied comparative religion and had taken some physics courses. A month after arriving at Purdue, she learned she would be teaching physics to naval officer students and to home economics students. In a 1995 taped interview, Anna said in her thick Viennese accent, "I had never heard of home economics. Who is going to tell me? My husband who had a PhD did not know what home economics was. So, I was told I should go to Miss Mary Matthews and get an explanation."

Mary told Anna what home economics students learned at Purdue. Anna said, "I had no idea that cooking and sewing—that a thing like that is taught." All home economics students were required to take physics, and the girls struggled with the course. Anna said, "The lab was a continuous stream of tears. They had hoped I would change that. I had one good idea in my life—change the course completely." Anna understood that the women were not interested in physics, but they did know of famous scientists like Newton and Galileo. Therefore, she introduced these famous men and others whom she called "astonishing human beings," then she taught the basics of physics. Anna's "one good idea" was a success. Anna taught in the Department of Physics for twenty-nine years, receiving College of Science honors for "Instructor of the Year" in 1966.

Jean Davis was hired to teach Freshman Clothing in 1944. She arrived in Lafayette on the James Whitcomb Riley train. Amy Howe, head of the Department of Clothing and Textiles, and Edith Gamble, head of the Department of Institutional Management, met her at the station and took her to lunch at McCord Candies in downtown Lafayette, a candy and soda shop that still exists today. Davis said, "One afternoon when I was sitting in the outer office waiting to go in and see Miss Matthews, Miss Gamble scurried in saying, 'Where's my brains? Where's my brains?!' Margaret Beeman explained to me that she [Gamble] always carried a little booklet to tell her what she had to do that day. Her little booklet was her brains."

Davis also told the story about the missing sugar from the RHI department during the World War II sugar shortage. Edith Gamble put a stop to those pilfering the sought-after staple by filling the sugar bags with salt.

Dean Emeritus Eva Goble was hired by Lella Gaddis to be a home demonstration agent in Terra Haute in 1941. She said, "Miss Gaddis was a very upright, fiery lady who thought we ought to do all we could to help women with better methods of managing their work. Of course that interested me because most of the state didn't have electricity yet, and farm women worked very hard. When I talked to Miss Gaddis, I thought now there's a woman I'd like to work for. She had real snappy eyes and you could see she wanted to get things done." During Goble's interview, Lella asked, "What makes you think you can do this job?" To which Goble replied in her youthful assurance, "I have never failed yet." Goble said, "She hired me, and I learned much from her."

A couple of years later, Goble was hired as a home management specialist on the Purdue campus. She was still new to the University when a letter came to her asking for nominations for a distinguished service award. Goble said, "I thought *I'll make two*, so I nominated Dean Matthews, who I thought did a beautiful job starting the school, and I nominated Miss Gaddis, who I thought did an outstanding job. It never occurred to me that they [Purdue] wouldn't treat both of these women the same. I learned about the University, because Dean Matthews was awarded the distinguished recognition, and Miss Gaddis, who was my boss, was not. I was horrified, as I had no idea that only one would be selected. Miss Gaddis very gallantly asked me to go to the ceremony with her in Elliott Hall. Miss Matthews came down from the stage and said, 'I understand I have you to thank for my being nominated.' And that's all I have to tell about that. How to get yourself into a hole."

The history shared by Goble and Mary Matthews makes the story even more interesting. When Goble was a home demonstration agent working for Lella in the Department of Agricultural Extension, she wanted to return to school for graduate work in home economics at Purdue, but Mary Matthews would not accept her into the school. Goble explained, "She said I didn't have enough science. She probably was right, but what she was doing was taking a slap at the Ag Boys. She said, 'I'm not going to educate their students if they don't let me have the money.' It all gets down to money." Goble "got around that stumbling block" with a visit to Dean Ernest Young, head of the graduate school. Goble explained, "He said, 'Oh, for Pete's sake. You can take any course you want, as long as you know how to do the work. He said engineers are looking for students right now in production engineering. Why don't you go over and get in engineering.' Well, I thought it wouldn't be bad—having an engineering degree. So, I went over there and took time and motion studies, which is the same thing you do in home economics. And, I got a B.S. in Home Economics, but I did it in engineering and agriculture. I only took one course in home economics."

While Goble worked for Lella, President Elliott's mother-in-law, Mrs. Nowland (who lived with her daughter and son-in-law on South 7th Street), would make regular visits to the campus. Goble said, "She was quite feeble at the time, but she would walk from Lafayette to West Lafayette. She would go around and visit all of the departments to be sure her son-in-law was doing the right thing. And Miss Gaddis was pretty smart [with her appointment]. She would always tell us, 'Now, the president's mother (in-law) is coming this afternoon. I don't want to be interrupted.' Miss Gaddis figured it out so that she came to us last, and Miss Gaddis took her home. She got her out of there."

Margaret Gustafson was a clerk stenographer in the extension office in 1940. She said, "I took shorthand. Then we used these machines (stenotype). Lella was a wonderful person. She talked very fast. It was hard to take dictation from her. Lella dictated letters to the home demonstration agents out in the state about all their projects and meetings."

Edith Hays was the first Ball State University graduate hired by Lella. She said, "It was really a thrilling experience to work with Miss Gaddis. She was an inspiration, and when she told me I was the first one from Ball State, I had to do right. I couldn't do otherwise." Often, home demonstration agents were asked to teach subjects about which they were not familiar but were willing to learn. Hays said, "They wanted a lesson on caning a chair. I bought an old chair and nearly broke my back learning how to cane this chair. I still have it. And, I happened to have a cousin who worked with Wayne Knitting Mills in Fort Wayne, and they produced the first nylon hose. I was able to show the first pair of nylon hose to a home demonstration group. I thought that was quite interesting."

Lella Gaddis sits in the homemade kitchen desk displayed in connection with the Home Economics Exhibit in the Purdue Building at the Indiana State Fair in September 1938. The sign in the background is appropriate, for Lella was a model of perfect posture. Courtesy of Purdue University Libraries, Archives and Special Collections.

At that time, Esther Hohlt Sohl interviewed with Lella for a home demonstration agent position. Sohl was married, which almost cost her a chance at the job. Lella did not think her agents should be married. She explained, "You need to devote every waking hour when you are an extension agent." Once Lella heard that Sohl's husband was to be sent overseas with the war effort, Lella consented to hiring her. Sohl said, "It wasn't my qualifications, but the fact that I was married."

Professor Emeritus Janalyce Rouls was a home demonstration agent in Kosciusko County for five years. She remembered what extension was like during the war. "(It) meant questioning what was being taught and to judge if it really contributed to the war effort, yet kept morale high," she said. "This was a difficult time for families, many of whom were loaning their men folks. We were going on meat, sugar, and gasoline rationing. Any time we started a car, people were asking, 'Is this trip necessary?'"

Rouls also talked of the overall contribution extension made to the family. She said, "I don't think we realize how the extension program has been interwoven into education for the whole family. I could see in our club program women who were very shy, modest, and unassuming rise to leadership ability, which in turn was passed on to their children. And then all of the kids wanted to come to Purdue for their education."

Anna K. Williams summed up the home demonstration extension effort. She said, "I'm grateful for working in the extension department for a total of thirty years. Miss Gaddis was our boss. She was a strong person who made us feel like we were going to change the world. And to some extent, I guess we really did."

❦

Mary Matthews wanted to strengthen the focus on child development and family relations in her school, so in 1946 she established the Department of Family Life. The other departments that year were the same five that began in 1926: Foods and Nutrition, Clothing and Textiles, Applied Design, Institutional Magagement, and Home Administration. The Department of Family Life included courses related to nursery school, including curricula regarding play, music, and books. Advanced courses in child development were offered along with courses on family health and relationships. Margaret Nesbit became the first head of the new department. Isabelle Diehl, who had been a wartime Army nurse and later received a master's degree from Purdue, joined the department and established innovative programs for infants and toddlers involving their mothers and Purdue students. Caroline McCullough was hired to be head teacher of the older children in the nursery school. She arranged for the Department of Family Life students to practice teaching kindergarten in public schools. The department established a cooperative nursery school for the children of professors and students, which later developed into the Nimitz Drive Nursery School. The department also developed a kindergarten for children of young faculty living in prefabricated housing on campus.

In an *Indianapolis Star* interview on June 14, 1947, Mary Matthews said, "Home Economics changes every five years, and we have to replan all the courses. I originated a course in housing, a study of room planning for efficiency. Through the years, I have put more emphasis on training in the management of money and time in the home. Also, I feel there is less need now for clothing construction and more for basic information on fabrics, their wearing qualities and their care." The article went on to state that Mary made postwar changes with special meal planning courses for wives living in barracks and trailers. There were about one thousand girls enrolled in her school at the time of the interview. That year, the school also offered a course combining home economics and engineering. She stated, "And we are gradually putting more and more attention on the art side of homemaking as well as the efficiency angle."

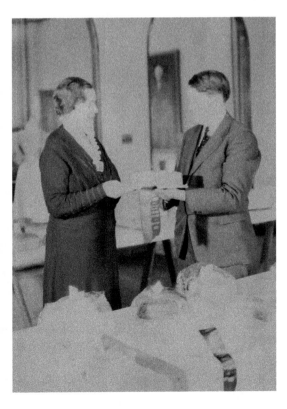

Dean Mary Matthews accepts a ribbon at the Indiana State Baking Contest in March 1934. She was said to be a gracious hostess, yet she did not especially like to cook. In 1947 under her tenure as dean, the famed Master Mix was developed at Purdue University under the direction of Professor Gertrude Sunderlin. Master Mix was the predecessor to all cake mixes available today. Courtesy of Purdue University Libraries, Archives and Special Collections.

What we know today as cake mix was developed at Purdue University. It was called "Master Mix," and students under the supervision of Gertrude Sunderlin created it in the home economics labs in 1947. Master Mix was a formulation of flour, baking powder, salt, cream of tartar, and shortening that could be prepared and stored for up to six weeks. It could be used to make cakes, pancakes, biscuits, and more at a savings of "75 percent of the usual mixing time." Master Mix was announced nationally in a 1947 issue of *Better Homes and Gardens* magazine in a three-page feature complete with recipes and photographs. The two students who had conducted most of the experimental work on the mix, Margaret Billings and Lucy Goetz, authored the story. Master Mix was also featured in a bulletin (HE 56) published by the Agricultural Extension Service. In 1950, after an interview about the revolutionary baking product was announced on the *Farm and Home Hour* radio broadcast on NBC Radio, 8,300 people made requests for copies. By 1952, the "Master Mix" bulletin was in its fourth printing and 75,000 copies had been produced, making it the fourth highest publication of any Purdue publication at the time. Letters poured into the Department of Foods and Nutrition, and women from all over the country described Master Mix as "an absolute necessity in every home."

Dean Emeritus Eva Goble said, "Gertrude Sunderlin had all the pastry people standing around waiting for her to finish it [Master Mix]. I had a man who was a specialist in wheat growing [from the Purdue Agricultural Department] come over and sit at my desk, and they were seeing it from a standpoint of getting their name on it." The School of Agriculture viewed Master Mix from the "wheat selling" perspective. The more Master Mix that was desired, the more wheat would be sold to manufacturers, and the more money the farmer would make. The women of the Department of Household Economics saw their creation as a laborsaving wonder rather than a means to sell more wheat.

After the initial success, Purdue students went on to develop other pre-prepared mixes like Homemade Cake and Cookie Mix, Gingerbread Mix, Spice Cake Mix, Chocolate Cake Mix, Pudding and Pie Filling Mix, and more, which were announced in national magazines such as *Woman's Day, Country Gentleman, Farm Journal,* and *Journal of the American Dietetic Association.*

A February 2, 1952 article in the Lafayette *Journal and Courier* stated, "Teachers, leaders of scout troops and 4-H clubs, commercial home economists, directors of institutions and even Canadian campers voiced their praise of this aid to good cooks. Even women in Ireland last summer inquired of Miss Ruth Carson, Purdue student and Indiana's international youth exchange representative, if she had helped with 'the Mix.' One homemaker said, "I don't know how I managed before I used the Mix."

Today, women can still find the recipe for Master Mix on www.cooks.com, which also features a passage written by the late Gertrude Sunderlin. She said, "The Master Mix recipes are time savers and reputation builders. The siftings and measuring of the dry ingredients and the blending of the fat can be done at one time for a dozen bakings."

Making the Master Mix

For 13 cups
9 cups sifted all-purpose flour or
10 cups sifted soft wheat or cake flour
1/3 cup double-acting baking powder
1 tablespoon salt
1 teaspoon cream of tartar
1/4 cup sugar
2 cups shortening which does not require refrigeration

Stir baking powder, salt, cream of tartar, and sugar into flour. Sift together three times into a large mixing bowl or onto a large square of plain paper. Cut into shortening until Mix is consistency of cornmeal. Store in covered containers at room temperature. To measure the Master Mix, pile it lightly into cup and level off with a spatula. If the Master Mix is to be used largely for cakes and cookies, starting with a box of cake flour will save measuring the flour and will give better textured products. For about 16 cups Mix, use a box of cake flour (2 3/4 pounds), 1/2 cup baking powder, 1 1/2 tablespoons salt, 1/4 cup sugar, and 1 pound shortening (2 1/3 cups).

Dying in a Light, White Blanket

Seven years are missing.

Kate Gaddis kept a diary for more than half of her life from 1906 to 1946. However, seven of her diaries have disappeared, making a gap of nearly a decade in the record of her days. As if the pause button was pushed between the years 1938 and 1944, the diaries have vanished and are not with their family of other leather-bound journals in the light blue shoebox that once held a pair of nurse's shoes. Readers are left wondering about the "lost years."

The great-niece of Kate and Lella Gaddis, Miriam Epple-Heath, is saddened by the disappearance of the journals. She explained the little she knows about the missing chronicles: "Several years ago, some of the diaries were taken by a relative and given to Duke University. Unfortunately, I don't know where they are now."

It is our loss. We cannot hear Kate's voice from 1938 to 1944. Yet perhaps it is for the best, because those were years of loss for Lella and Kate.

After teaching for fifty years, Kate retired in June 1939 at age seventy. She was probably ready to stay home and putter around the house. Her diabetes and thyroid problems caused an array of health issues, and it was time to stop teaching. This was the year Lella traveled to London to attend the meeting of the Associated Country Women.

She spent several weeks touring Europe to study homemaking problems in various countries. It is not known if Kate accompanied Lella and recorded the trip in one of her leather-bound books that is now gone.

In 1940, the Gaddis sisters' nephew, Paul, died at his home at the age of forty-six. Paul had lived with Lella and Kate when he was a Purdue student. He and Lella began classes together the same year. Paul was the son Lella and Kate never had, and he was the only child of their sister Mamie. At the time of his death, Paul owned the Riley Poultry Farm at the north edge of West Lafayette, and he had worked for Allied Mills. A heavy smoker, Paul had been ill for thirteen months with heart trouble. The obituary in the Lafayette *Journal and Courier* states, "He was considered one of the leading poultry breeders of the United States."

Miriam Epple-Heath is the widow of Paul's son, Robert. She said, "Paul died on Christmas day. They sent the children to a movie that afternoon to get them out of the tenseness." At the time, Robert was a sophomore at Purdue and was a member of the Purdue basketball team. His sister, Mary Louise, was a senior at Purdue, and another sister, Virginia Lois, was a senior at West Lafayette High School across the street from Lella and Kate's home on Grant Street. Paul was survived by his parents, Mamie and Henry, and his wife, Ruth. Ruth took over the operation of the poultry farm with help from her children.

A coworker at Allied Mills wrote this tribute to Paul Riley: "Above all, he was a builder of men. His own salesmen loved him because he was a leader, because he was fair in his way of handling problems, because he was honest and unselfish in motive and would fight for and defend them against criticism. He was a true friend and helped many a man grow to his full stature."

Three years later, Paul's parents celebrated their fiftieth wedding anniversary with an open house at Trinity United Methodist Church in Lafayette, and Lella and Ruth presided over the refreshment table. It had been a half a century since the couple married in the residence of the Tippecanoe County Jail where William Gaddis had been sheriff. The table was covered with the white, linen damask cloth that had been given to the couple as a wedding gift from Margaret Gaddis, the mother of Mamie, Lella, Kate, and their late brother, Clyde. In the story from the *Journal and Courier*, there was no mention of Kate attending the golden anniversary celebration. As was the custom in ear-lier days, the story included a listing of some of the attendees who had signed the party registry. Kate's name was not on the list. She would have been seventy-three; perhaps she was ill that day.

⟜ ⟶ ⟵ ⟝

In Kate's diaries, the year 1937 left off with Lella seeing "Friend Dave" on a regular basis. Each month, Kate recorded when Lella ate supper with David Ross or when the sisters paid him a visit for a weekend stay at his country home, The Hills. Few people knew of the special rela-tionship shared by Lella and Ross. In *Ross-Ade: Their Purdue Stories, Stadium, and Legacies*, Robert C. Kriebel writes of what visitors experi-enced when they stayed with Ross: "He rose each day at 6:30 a.m. He loved having recorded music—later commercial radio music—going from the crack of dawn. He enjoyed card games. . . . However he was not to be disturbed if he retired to a workshop or drafting table where he might flesh out sudden brainstorms."

On July 16, 1942, seventy-one-year-old Ross was to preside at a meeting and banquet of the National Farm Chemurgic Council at Purdue. However, just prior to the event, he turned his plans over to his secretary and drove to The Hills. A few hours later, he collapsed from a stroke, which resulted in paralysis on one side of his body. It rendered Ross unable to speak and without the use of one arm and leg. At the time, Ross was president of the Purdue University Board of Trustees. He remained on the board *in absentia*. Ross lived for eleven months in a paralyzed state until he died in his home on South 7th Street on June 18, 1943. Kate's missing diary could have told readers so much more. Did Lella visit and care for this kind, brilliant, gener-ous man who was left unable to speak or walk? How did the traumatic turn of events impact Lella? Did Ross's death along with the death of her beloved nephew a few years before change her in noticeable ways? Miriam Epple-Heath said, "Lella was very guarded about him [Ross]. She didn't talk about it." We are left to our imaginations. However, this much we know: to Purdue and the world, David Ross was a legend in his own time. For Lella, he was "Friend Dave."

Ross was not a churchgoer, but his funeral was held at Central Presbyterian Church in downtown Lafayette. This was the church where Lella and Kate had been members since the early 1900s and faithfully attended "SS [Sunday school] and worship" as Kate recorded in her diaries nearly every Sunday. If the sisters did not attend church, Kate wrote, "We were lazy and did not go." The Reverend William R. Graham was the renowned preacher there, and he conducted Ross's funeral. After the funeral, Ross's sealed casket was moved to the Purdue Research Foundation campus, to which Ross was a major contributor, on West Stadium Avenue in West Lafayette. Purdue closed that day from 2 p.m. to 4 p.m. so that faculty and students could attend the memorial program. Honorary pallbearers included Indiana Governor Henry F. Schricker and President Edward Elliott. Students carried the casket of David Ross as tribute to his many efforts to help young people reach their goals.

Ross left most of his estate, which was valued at more than two million dollars, to Purdue, Home Hospital, and to several of his relatives. He gave the city of West Lafayette twelve acres of land along the Wabash River between State and Brown Streets. In his will, Ross bequeathed "The Hills" with his summer home and 197 acres to the Purdue Research Foundation.

At his request, Ross was buried at one of his favorite places on campus, a knoll north of Stadium Avenue on land he had given to the Purdue Research Foundation. Eleven acres were dedicated for a David Ross Memorial, today near Slayter Center. Carved into the granite slab that covers his grave are these words:

David E. Ross, 1871-1943
Dreamer, Builder, Faithful Trustee
Creator of Opportunity for Youth

The Lafayette *Journal and Courier* ended the article about the death of David Ross with these words: "Mr. Ross never married, and he is survived only by a sister, Mrs. Mary G. Stidham of Oakland, California."

❦

Fast-forward from 1937 to 1945, and there was a shift in Kate's writing topics and the tenor of her words. She was seventy-nine when she sat by the library window in the home she still shared with Lella on Grant Street across from West Lafayette High School and wrote in her 1945 diary. Her last years were spent in a wheelchair. Kate was not well, and Lella had hired Mrs. Barrett, whom they called Mrs. B., to care for

Kate and the house while she was at work. Kate recorded what she saw outside, often repeating each day the same scenarios and worries. She writes:

> February 21: Lella left for the north part of the state. Rains all day, too. Dear, oh dear. I worry so about Lella. All I can do is pray for her safe return.
>
> March 10: I see by the church program that the church is open as anyone can go in for a few minutes mediation. I wish I could. But I can't, so will have to meditate at home.
>
> March 20: I do try to be patient as I sit here day in and day out. I do worry a lot, and I don't believe it helps much.
>
> March 30: Jess Browning was found dead in her apartment. That is a fine way to go, and I do hope I can go that way. I must not worry Lella.
>
> April 7: A teachers affair at Purdue today. Oh, how I would like to go, but I can only sit at home and knit and read. Dear, oh, dear, how depressed I feel.

During this time, sixty-eight-year-old Lella did not travel as often for her extension work as she did in the early years. She worked more in her office at Purdue, and on most days, she came home to have lunch with Kate. When she did travel, she drove a Purdue "extension car," rode a bus, or took the train. Kate's post at the library window provided her with a place to watch her bird feeder and the neighbors, the Redfields. She wrote down when Mr. Redfield took in his garbage cans and when Mrs. Redfield had "wash day," for she saw the laundry hanging on the line to dry. There were coal strikes reported in the news. Kate worried that she and Lella would run out of coal for their furnace and commented on each coal delivery they received. She still kept up with current events, particularly the end of World War II:

> February 15: The terrible war. Will it ever end? I get so worried about things. Am so glad I have my retirement and Lella has her job. We have this home all paid for and rent money each month coming in.

> April 13: President Roosevelt died yesterday of cerebral hemorrhage. Vice President Truman was sworn in last night.

> April 19: Ernie Pyle, the war writer, killed by a Jap yesterday. Mrs. B. very excited. I, myself, had never heard of him.

Ernie Pyle was a journalist from Dana, Indiana, who wrote as a roving correspondent for the Scripps-Howard newspaper chain from 1935 until his death in combat during World War II. He wrote with a folksy style, as if he were writing a personal letter to a friend. His articles appeared in more than three hundred newspapers. In 1928, he became the country's first aviation columnist. Amelia Earhart said, "Any aviator who didn't know Pyle was a nobody." Pyle became a war correspondent and applied his intimate style to the conflict. Pyle generally wrote from the perspective of the common soldier, an approach that won him not only further popularity, but also a 1944 Pulitzer Prize. Kate notes:

> May 5: VE Day. Germany has surrendered. I do hope this terrible war is coming to an end. They haven't' found Hitler, but think he is dead.

> May 8: This is President Harry Truman's 51 birthday. They move into the White House. We have had wonderful radio programs from all over the world. The President suggests that Sunday, Mother's Day, be a day of thanksgiving and prayer, as he says Japan has to be beaten and the war only half over.

President Edward Elliott retired from Purdue after having turned the mandatory retirement age of seventy the previous December. Upon his retirement, the Purdue University Board of Trustees created the office of "President Emeritus." Lella attended the University party honoring the Elliotts before their departure. Dean A. A. Potter was named interim president until Frederick L. Hovde took office in January of 1946.

Lella and Kate were close to their late nephew's three children. Robert brought his fiancée by the house to meet his great-aunts before he went off to war. This visit was like a flashback to the day in 1917 when Robert's father, Paul, brought by his girl, Ruth, before he went off to the World War I. The sisters worried for Paul when he was flying in the first war, and then they worried about his son fighting in the second war. Robert's fiancée was Miriam Epple-Heath. Kate writes:

> June 25: Robert and his girl here for awhile. She with a lovely diamond. She seems like such a fine girl.

> July 26: I hope Robert gets out of this war ok. There have been so many casualties.

> August 8: They used a terrific bomb on the Japs called atom bomb.

> August 10: The Japs have decided to quit fighting.

> August 11: In tonight's paper, picture of Miriam and her announcement of her and Robert's engagement. Now if he gets home safe and sound. Miriam is a good-looking girl.

> August 15: Japs surrender. Such good news last night. The Japs Surrendred. Last night, bells rang and whistles blew. I remember when World War 1 ended. It was in November. Hope Robert gets home soon.

Miriam Kline was a student in Purdue's School of Home Economics when she became engaged to Robert Riley. The couple planned to marry before Miriam graduated, but her father was not pleased. He wanted her to graduate first. He threatened that he would not walk her down the aisle, but he changed his mind with persuasion from Miriam's mother. Miriam was staying at the Practice House at the time. With her father's negative attitude toward the engagement heavy on her mind, encouragement came knocking at the door, literally. Miriam remembered that moment: "There was Lella all dressed up, and she said, 'I have an engagement gift for you.'" Lella handed Miriam a copy of the *Ladies' Home Journal Cookbook* she still uses today.

For years, Lella and Kate hired women to come to their home and do their laundry and cleaning. During this time, they hired a laundry service, and Kate recorded each time the deliveryman arrived at their door. They were having trouble finding a housekeeper. Mrs. Barrett's main job was to be on hand for Kate and make her meals. One woman they hired to clean wanted to smoke, and the Gaddis sisters would not allow it, so she quit. Lella tended to the house between housekeepers. Kate said, "Lella taking a few days vacation. Working like a fiend here at home. I can't help it if she does. She always had a mind of her own. I used to think I was the boss, but not anymore. I don't know what I am here for anyway."

Kate continued to read the latest in literature, and when she commented on her reading during this time, the younger Kate shone through. She read *Green Dolphin Street* and wrote, "It is some story, and so fine one can hardly read it." *Green Dolphin Street*, by Elizabeth Goudge, was first published in Britain in 1944. It was the story of a young man in 1800s New Zealand who sends for the woman he loves who lives in the British Isles. Inadvertently, he addresses his letter to her sister with whom he also shares a past. It became a top movie in 1947 staring Lana Turner, Van Heflin, and Donna Reed. Later, the theme song to the movie became a Miles Davis jazz classic.

Robert returned home from the war in the fall. The sisters were so thankful he was safe and not wounded. Robert and Miriam were married on December 22, and Kate described the ceremony as "such a lovely wedding." It was Christmastime, and Lella made her traditional fruitcake and persimmon pudding. Kate was still in touch with their friend, former coworker, and boarder, Anna Roberta McNeill Whitton, whom she had visited in Canada many years before. The next year Mack, her husband, and son even paid the women a visit.

The following January, Kate mentioned Mary Matthews and Eva Goble, who Lella would hire as a Vigo County home demonstration agent and who later would become her successor. Lella had to obtain consent from Leroy Hoffman, associate director of Agricultural Extension, to hire Goble as an extra home demonstration agent at the time. As the month progressed, more trials were in store. Lella must have worried for both of her sisters, Mamie and Kate, as she worked and traveled.

> January 3: I hope Lella gets to keep Eva Goble. A note from Miss Matthews telling what a nice girl Miriam is.

January 14: I fainted in the bathroom. Have a terrible banged up eye. Stayed in bed all day. They took Mamie to the hospital, the place she should be.

January 27: Mamie is very ill.

January 28: I think Mamie is very low. She can't last long.

January 29: Mamie died this morning. She had been in the hospital 2 weeks.

Mamie was eighty when she passed away, and her funeral was at Trinity United Methodist Church. Kate attended her sister's service with a bruise on her eye. She said a handful of people attended, including Mamie's widowed husband, Henry. Many of the women's friends in the community and at Purdue were dying at this time, and Kate said, "I wonder who of our friends will be next."

In the months that followed, Henry caused the family worry with his erratic behavior. On March 30, he fell and broke his hip. He died three days later. Lella and Ruth, Henry's sister-in-law and daughter-in-law, selected Henry's casket and planned his funeral. Kate records the sad day on April 4, "Henry's funeral today at Trinity. They had a lovely service. So, that is the end of Henry and Mamie on this earth. Poor old Henry was not accountable for what he did after Mamie's death."

❧

Due to rationing during the war, women's silk stockings disappeared from the market. When the war ended, they became available on a limited basis. Kate writes:

February 6: The paper says each woman will be allowed ten pair of stocking a year. I am sure I can get along with that way. You can't get a pair now.

March 25: Lella went to Indianapolis. She sent ten pairs of stockings home from Ayres [L.S. Ayres department store] in this morning's mail. So glad she found them. She needed them badly.

Lella and Kate attended an Art Club dinner in the spring, and the guest speaker was Randolph Coats, the Brown County artist who painted Lella's portrait six years earlier.

During this time, the women had a student boarder and handyman named Dick. One day he brought the sisters a gift, which Kate records on March 24: "Dick brings home the *Life of Mr. Ross* for us to read. We certainly did have a good many nice times down at The Dave's. Dave Ross was a fine man."

One of Kate's very first diary entries in 1906 was a comment about the "Little Skinner" arriving in the night. That baby was John Skinner, Jr., son of John H. Skinner, dean of the School of Agriculture. In the early years, Lella babysat for the "Little Skinner." In her final diary of 1946, Kate wrote that John Skinner, Jr. had a baby boy. Yet another "Little Skinner" was born, and Lella and Kate reveled in the newborn who felt to them like one of their own.

That summer, Kate commented that it was "Flying Farmers Day." She said, "You never heard so much flying." On December 12, 1945, the National Flying Farmers Association was incorporated in Oklahoma. It was made up of a group of farmers who used airplanes in their fieldwork. By air, they checked livestock, crop conditions, or irrigation systems, hauled supplies, or traveled between the farm and the parts store. Today it is the International Flying Farmers Association.

In her final diary, Kate continued to repeat her worries of running out of coal for the furnace and the safety of Lella when she traveled. She often wrote, "Oh, dear," and apparently she frequently vocalized those words, to Mrs. Barratt's chagrin:

> August 3: Mrs. B. sparked up this morning. So now, I don't dare say, "Oh, dear," in her presence. I guess, I can think it.

> August 15: Lella gone for the day. I think I will just worry myself to death. I wish I could. I can't talk to Mrs. B. She don't want me to say anything to her. So gloomy and dark. Oh, dear.

Yet Kate perked up on some days and continued to read her books and knit. She still had her sense of humor, as well, noting, for example, on November 13, "H. J. [Reed] stopped for me at noon, and I went over there for lunch. Amy Lord and Dean Matthews there. Miss Matthews could not start her car. Out of gas. Even a Buick will not run without gas."

Christmas Eve 1946 arrived, and the sisters attended a party at the Riley's home. Kate wore a new dress. She wrote her usual "Santa certainly good to us," but then it was as if she had a premonition:

> December 27: We have so much Christmas. The couch in the library is full. Seems to me it is a sad Christmas. I should be ashamed, and I am.

> December 29: Snowing this morning. The year seems to be dying in a light white blanket. Only three more days of this year, then comes a new one. Then, what? No one knows.

⟨~∾∾⟩

Bertha Kate Gaddis passed away on June 6, 1947, at the age of seventy-eight. She was buried in Springvale Cemetery on State Road 25, Lafayette, Indiana. She was survived by her sister, Lella.

Spirit of Twin Pines

In 1947, Lella Gaddis retired from the job she had created and performed with zeal, and for the first time in her seventy years, she no longer had her sister, Kate, to share her home and her life. Lella retired as state leader of home demonstration, having reached Purdue's mandatory retirement age in May, less than a month before Kate passed away. Lella had served Purdue, Indiana, and Hoosier women for thirty-four years. At the time of Lella's retirement, she was responsible for home demonstration agents in fifty-six counties, and they served nearly fifty thousand women in Home Economics Clubs around the state. The Indiana Home Economics Association (IHEA) established the Lella R. Gaddis Scholarship that year. The purpose of the scholarship was to promote the study of home economics and was to be given to a freshman in Purdue's School of Home Economics. Recipients were selected at the Indiana State Fair School for Girls. In the fiftieth anniversary commemorative booklet for the Indiana Home Demonstration Association, printed in 1963, it states, "At the State Fair School for Girls, the most valuable and esteemed scholarship is the Lella R. Gaddis Scholarship."

At the annual business meeting of the IHEA in January, Lella presented the idea of the association sponsoring a cooperative house for girls majoring in home economics at Purdue. She liked the concept of a house where girls could live and work together to reduce the costs of an education. Dean Emeritus Eva Goble, Lella's successor, said, "Lella talked to the state leader in Oregon. They were building a co-op house. She thought it was such a wonderful idea. It was getting so expensive to send girls to college. This was a way to get more girls up here."

It was suggested that the building be fully equipped and furnished to house twenty to thirty girls. The women wanted to vote immediately, but Lella asked the members to think it over, appoint a committee, and return to the next annual meeting ready to discuss the possibilities. Also at that meeting, a motion was made to hold the annual IHEA meeting in the summer, rather than January. Since that vote, the meeting has been held every summer at Purdue University.

The next year at the annual meeting, the cooperative house project was officially adopted, and the question of fund-raising was discussed. One woman moved that each delegate take the idea for the "Live at Home and Learn House" to her club and raise $1 per member. By 1950, nearly $18,000 had been raised. The next year, Lella hosted a breakfast for the past presidents, and each woman was to bring $10 for the endeavor. The total funds reached nearly $21,000, and it was decided to loan the money to the Purdue Research Foundation, under the direction of R. B. Stewart, who would help seek a house. Goble said, "Miss Gaddis retired. I got the job of getting it done. So, I went to R. B. Stewart, because I thought R. B. had more handles on things than most people. He was the controller. I explained to him that the women were digging up this money with the idea of getting a house. He said, 'I think it's a wonderful idea. What do you want me to do?' I said, 'Well, I need help finding a house.'"

With the consent of the IHEA's Cooperative House Committee, the foundation purchased a lot and house at 322 Waldron Street in West Lafayette. Mary Matthews lived up the street at 629 Waldron. The first Home Management House to be established was still operating at 115 Waldron. The street was a "hotbed" of home economics synergy. In 1952-1953, ten girls lived in the co-op house during remodeling. Stewart had some physical plant men who he said "weren't very busy," and he told Goble, "You get your girls to plan what they think it [the house] ought to look like, and our men will do it [renovation] for them." Rent from the girls would pay the additional needed money that was mortgaged. During the construction, Home Demonstration Clubs throughout the state raised another $8,000 for furnishings. Members of the Home Demonstration Chorus purchased a spinet piano for the house. A couple of years later, the IHEA named the house "Twin Pines" as a symbol of cooperation. There was even a song written, "She's a Twin Pines Girl," which was to be sung to the tune of "You're a Grand Old Flag":

> She's a Twin Pines girl; she's the best in the world,
> And she's known for her sweet, friendly smile.
> Her heart is true, and loyal, too, for she is a girl from
> TWIN PINES.
>
> Oh the house she chose is the best cause she knows
> That the girls live in sisterhood.
> You'll not forget her once you have met her,
> for she is a TWIN PINES girl.

Goble said, "One of the old boys who was always throwing stabs at everything we did said there wasn't a pine tree in sight. I can't remember his name. He was always mad at us about something." In 1959, money was collected to landscape the house, and two pine trees were planted. Thirty years later, vandals cut down the large pine trees that flanked the co-op, so during homecoming that year, a dedication ceremony was held for two new pine trees donated by the Indiana Extension Homemakers Association to replace the mutilated trees.

In fall of 1954, Twin Pines Cooperative officially opened to house twenty-four women. It was formally dedicated at the IHEA Conference the previous June. A plaque was presented to the first group of women to live in the house. The plaque reads:

> To honor Lella Reed Gaddis for 34 years of service,
> The Indiana Home Demonstration Association dedicates
> Twin Pines Cooperative House, June 18, 1954.

Tours were held during the conference and many conferences after so that all homemakers from Indiana could see the results and feel a part of what they had helped to accomplish. Goble said, "We were all real proud of it. The county presidents stayed there during conferences."

The first housemother was Edith Soper, who was a counselor, a guide to the girls, and a gracious host. She served Twin Pines for ten years. Goble said, "Mom Soper was the housemother, and she was a blessing. She knew exactly how to manage things."

Today, Twin Pines Cooperative is open to young women from all majors. In the fiftieth anniversary commemorative booklet printed in 2002, it recapped the essence of the fortieth anniversary celebration: "Everyone was reminded of what it means to be a Twin Pines girl and realized that the Twin Pines spirit was still alive."

Lella's mark still floats among the pines, helping women to become their all.

❦

Once Lella retired and took stock of her life without Kate, she reveled in the arts and traveling. She spent time with her great-nephew, Robert Riley, his wife Miriam, and their three children. Lella traveled to Hawaii and other far-off places, collecting travel posters along the way. She created beautiful woodcarvings including an ornate wood screen and a double fireplace mantle that the Riley family still treasures today. She enjoyed china painting and making wool-braided rugs, a craft she had demonstrated to many Indiana women. She signed her china and other art pieces with the letters "LRG," making her initials her logo. Lella did needlepoint, and she made exquisite kid (goat leather) gloves as gifts. Even in her seventies, she modeled in fashion shows for Alpha Chi Omega Sorority, walking with her signature erect posture. Miriam Epple-Heath remembers seeing her great-aunt in a fashion show. Miriam thought, "Oh, to be a lady like that." Lella traveled to Indianapolis and Chicago where she would buy "Hill and Dale" brand shoes and "Mountain Home" brand dresses. When she departed for a shopping excursion, she said, "I feel like I have to get the moss off my back." She still called her car the "machine," and in her retirement, she drove a yellow 1957 Chevrolet the family named the "yellow canary."

Lella continued to entertain and host wedding rehearsal dinners for friends and family. At the time, her elegant dinners would include such guests as Earl Butz, dean of the School of Agriculture, Dave Pfendler, assistant dean of the School of Agriculture, and Mrs. Reed, wife of the late Harry Reed, dean of the School of Agriculture. She

Even in retirement, Lella Gaddis did not let the grass grow under her feet. Just like in her home demonstration extension days, she traveled, except now to far-off lands rather than Indiana back roads. In the above photograph, she is ready to leave Indiana for California and on to Hawaii in 1955. Courtesy of Miriam Epple-Heath.

gave each baby born into the family a child-size stainless flatware set from Sweden and a savings bond. For each birthday after, she gave additional savings bonds. Family was important to Lella. She was like a beloved mother-in-law to Miriam. In the 1960s, Lella spent a great deal of time with Robert and Miriam. They would pick Lella up every Sunday, squeeze her in the back seat with their three children, attend church, and then she would share Sunday dinner at their home. Lella loved her great-great-nieces and nephew, and when she accompanied Miriam to the grocery store, she presided over the cart, pushing her great-great-niece as if she were her mother. When little Joan fussed, wanting something in the store, Lella told her, "It's just like going to the bargain sale, without funds." Whenever anyone asked Lella why she never married, she replied, "I have spent 85% of my time waiting for a man to keep appointments on time. I'm not going to give up the other 15%."

Lella still lived on Grant Street across from West Lafayette High School. She would have Miriam's son, Guy, over for lunch when he attended there. She fed him oyster stew, with nary an oyster. Lella was still frugal, and her years of teaching Indiana women how to conserve and preserve during World Wars I and II remained part of her core. She reused foil and waxed paper. She still had her homes for rent on Russell Street, and she took in faculty and students as boarders. She kept the rent low, never raising the prices. She said, "I like the caliber of people I have, and I don't want to drive them out." Lella remained steady with her candor and fearless in her ways. One day, she was about to pull her yellow canary machine into a parking spot at the grocery store when another driver pulled in ahead of her. Lella got out of her car, walked up to the person, and said, "Someone should give you a courtesy card."

In the early 1960s while attending Purdue, Ralph Neill lived in a room in Lella's home in exchange for work and chauffeur duties. Neill worked ten hours a week doing yard work and minor repairs. He drove the yellow canary he termed "one neat, classy vehicle" and took Lella, then in her eighties, where she needed to go. In 2010, Neill said, "Instead of *Driving Miss Daisy*, I drove Miss Gaddis." He took her shopping, to the cemetery, to the movies, and to Twin Pines Cooperative functions. In return, Lella provided Neill with a room and breakfast. Neill said, "The breakfast was first-rate to say the very least. If I was working on Saturday, she invited me in for lunch. Well, her cooking was so splendid; I tried my best to find something to do each and every Saturday!"

Neill describes Lella in this way: "She was an elegant and very proud person. Outwardly, she tried to be very stern, but inwardly, she was very soft, gentle, and most kind. I remember my two years with Lella Gaddis with much affection and warmth. I certainly received more than I expected, and I hope she felt the same."

In her late eighties, Lella became even thriftier. She often walked from her home on Grant Street to the Purdue Memorial Union for dinner in the cafeteria. Lella tended not to eat well, so the family had "Meals on Wheels," a mission service provided by Trinity Methodist Church, deliver food to her door. But Lella would save the food instead of eating it. The woman who had taught thousands of Hoosiers about growing vegetable gardens, food preparation, and food preserva-

In her later years, Lella Gaddis spent time with her great nephew, Robert Gaddis Riley, his wife, Miriam, and their children, Gail, Jane, and Guy (not pictured). In the above photograph, Robert celebrates his thirty-ninth birthday in 1960. He was the son of Paul Gaddis Riley, the nephew to whom Lella and her sister Kate were also quite fond. Courtesy of Miriam Epple-Heath.

tion did not want to accept help. One day she called Miriam and said, "Oh, I did a terrible thing. I singed my hair." Miriam rushed to her house and found that Lella had been warming her clothes in front of the open gas oven. The clothes caught fire, and Lella's hair and face were singed. The family decided Lella could not be alone, and they hired a woman to live with her.

As time progressed, Lella had memory and health issues, and the family moved her into the Indiana Pythian Home on South 18th Street in Lafayette. The immense red brick building was constructed in 1927. The Indiana Pythian Home is nestled among trees in a park-like setting. Today the building is in disrepair, and its future is in question. After the family moved Lella to the home, they were told they could not visit for two weeks. When Miriam and her family were finally able to make their first visit to their great-aunt, they found her sitting in the massive lobby. As they sat there together, Lella looked around and said, "The woodwork is beautiful. It's like the Purdue Memorial

Union woodwork." To the end, Purdue was the fire that fueled Lella's days.

Lella Reed Gaddis died on January 16, 1968, at the age of eighty-nine. She had been ill for three weeks in the Indiana Pythian Home where she had been a resident for one year. Lella was buried in Spring-vale Cemetery on State Road 25, Lafayette, Indiana, next to her parents, William Alfred and Margaret Elizabeth Reed Gaddis, and her sister, Bertha Kate Gaddis.

Mary L. Matthews Club

The news came click clicking over the Associated Press teletype machine to WOWO Radio in Fort Wayne, Indiana, on December 7, 1951. Mary L. Matthews, dean of the School of Home Economics at Purdue University, would retire the following January after forty-one years as a member of the University staff. Like Lella Gaddis, Mary would leave after reaching Purdue's mandatory retirement age of seventy. At the time of Mary's retirement, Purdue's School of Home Economics was the second largest in land-grant colleges. Mary's retirement year was filled with teas, lunches, and banquets to honor her as the outgoing dean. In January, the home economics staff hosted a dinner in the south ballroom of the Purdue Memorial Union, the edifice Mary's mother had pushed to fruition so many years before. Lella attended. Dignitaries spoke. President Frederick L. Hovde lauded Mary as "our gracious and distinguished lady." President Emeritus Edward Elliott deemed her "the great mistress of duty in the home." Dean of the School of Agriculture Harry Reed told the crowd, "Agriculture in Indiana is richer because of her service." Dean A. A. Potter, Mary's trusted ally, said, "We are honoring a colleague who has contributed richly to an appreciation of the art of homemaking." Potter closed the evening with these words: "Dean Matthews has started at Purdue University a chain reaction in better and happier living for humanity."

Mary was featured in an article in the January 1952 *Purdue Alumnus* magazine. The newsletter for the Purdue University chapter of Pi Beta Phi, "The Tiny Arrow," featured a story uplifting her endeavors to create their chapter house and make it one of the leading groups on campus. The chapter house hosted a party for Mary. The group gave her a purse as a retirement gift, and the president of the association said, "We are glad you wear the flower of Pi Beta Phi today." Mary was lauded at the Parent-Teacher Association Founders Day dinner in February for her thirty years of service to the Indiana Congress of Parents and Teachers. In his tribute, Allan A. Smith said, "I heard this great friend and outstanding community leader, Lillian Stewart, quote Dean Matthews by saying, 'Service is the rent you pay for occupying space'. It seems more applicable to Dean Mary than anyone whom I can consider at this time, the phrase 'the luxury of being used.'"

Mary was honored at a Purdue tea where she was presented with a silver tray. In April, then Professor Eva Goble was chairman of an agricultural staff luncheon to celebrate Mary. The event was held in the north ballroom of the Purdue Memorial Union, and the cost was $1.35 per person. One hundred and thirty agricultural staff members attended. Dean of the School of Agriculture Harry Reed made tribute to Mary's pioneering work in home economics. The Tippecanoe County Home Demonstration Chorus, under the direction of Al Stewart, provided entertainment.

In May, Mary attended a Purdue University Board of Trustees luncheon. David Ross was present at this event. He would fall victim to a stroke two months later. At the banquet held the prior January, Dean A. A. Potter had said, "To our colleague, Dean Matthews, should go much of the credit for the present standing of home economics at Purdue University. Credit should also be given to two great Trustees, Virginia C. Meredith and David E. Ross. Both Mrs. Meredith and Mr. Ross had a full awareness of the importance of home economics as a career, and of its place in the land-grant university."

Mary was invited to act as marshal at commencement exercises that year, and she led the faculty in the academic procession outdoors and into the Hall of Music. The festivities surrounding her departure must have been special to Mary for she kept a scrapbook of her retirement events. Inside are announcements, invitations, clippings, and remembrances. Today the scrapbook is preserved in the Purdue Uni-

Dean Mary L. Matthews (far right) stands on the steps of the Home Economics Building (later named Matthews Hall) at Purdue University with members of the Parent-Teacher Association during Parents' Institute, November 3 and 4, 1937. Courtesy of Professor Emeritus Mary Louise Foster.

versity Virginia Kelly Karnes Archives and Special Collections Research Center. When her retirement was announced in December of 1951, the Purdue *Exponent* devoted an entire issue to Mary and the School of Home Economics. The editorial that day closed with these words: "The work of Dean Mary L. Matthews will not soon be forgotten. She will remain for years to come the symbol of advancement in the field of Home Economics education."

President Hovde toyed with the idea of appointing a man to be Mary's successor. He once admitted that he failed to achieve significant change in the School of Home Economics, and he said, "It was the one academic area at Purdue that stumped me." Instead, he appointed Beulah V. Gillaspie who had headed home economics at the University of Arkansas. As much as Mary was a reserved "lady" with her tightly coifed hair, sensible shoes, and scarf knotted at the collar, almost like a necktie, Gillaspie was forward, in a "New York" way (sometimes described as "pushy"), and she liked fashion. She had worked as an editor and director of the laboratory kitchen for *McCall's* magazine in New York City. Dean Emeritus Eva Goble said, "Beulah was right out of business. Her job was to increase the students to get into business. I think she made a contribution there. She was a fancy dresser. The kids loved it. She wore a sleeve of bracelets and high-heeled shoes. They just thought she was great. They could see what they had to do if they were going to go into business. She grew up in a river town in Pennsylvania. And she had to forge her way, and believe me, by the time you move a bunch of trunks around, catch buses, and get on airplanes, you get pushy. So I guess she was teaching them something she thought they needed to know."

Goble said that Gillaspie was wooed to Purdue with the promise of a new building. She was able to put her mark on the Home Economics Administration Building, now Stone Hall. During the building's construction, two huge mountains of dirt stood at the site, which students named Mount Hovde for President Frederick Hovde, and Mount Stewart for Vice President R. B. Stewart. In 1986, Dean Emeritus Gillaspie recounted, "They said you could walk between the mountains into Beulah Land. I thought it was great. I even received mail addressed that way."

Just as Mary Matthews retired in 1952, Purdue took home economics education to South America. Through Purdue's Technical Assistance Program, home economics "technicians" from Purdue helped to establish a School of Home Economics at the Rural University of Minas Gerais in Vicosa, Brazil—the first in South America to grant a bachelor's degree in home economics. Dean Emeritus Eva Goble served as the first home economics consultant on the project, hiring staff and initiating the first college home economics courses. By the 1960s, the Brazilian government recognized home economics as a profession, and Purdue's involvement in the project ended in 1965. For Mary, who had developed the School of Household Economics from the early years, and Lella, who had hired Eva Goble as a home demonstration agent and to be her successor, the Brazil project was a new frontier that was also their milestone. The two women had built the foundation of Purdue home economics and extension, and the Brazil project took that foundation globally.

After Mary retired, a Home Economics Club was formed in her name on March 3, 1952. The minutes from the first meetings of the Mary L. Matthews Club are in a cranberry-hued, leather-bound book, larger, yet similar in antiquated look and feel to the diaries of Kate Gaddis. Inside are the constitution and bylaws of the club. Dues were $1.50 per year. Minutes of the organizational meeting state, "This club will be affiliated with the County Federation of Women's Clubs and will have as its object the study of Modern Trends in 20th Century Living." Programs were to include various types of talks, book reviews, and demonstrations. The first program meeting was held later that month at Mary's home on Waldron Street. The daffodil was chosen as the club flower. Edith Gamble was one of the charter members. She had been Mary's assistant in the Department of Household Economics. The club also gave to various causes like the American Red Cross and the "Polio Fund." Every meeting began with the members standing to "pray" "A Collect for Club Women," which was written by Mary Stewart:

Keep us, oh God, from pettiness; let us be large in thought, in word, in deed.

Let us be done with fault-finding and leave off self-seeking.

May we put away all pretense and meet each other face to face —without self-pity and without prejudice.

May we never be hasty in judgment and always generous.

Let us take time for all things; make us to grow calm, serene, gentle.

Teach us to put into action our better impulses, straightforward, and unafraid.

Grant that we may realize it is the little things that create differences, that in the big things of life we are at one.

And may we strive to touch and to know the great, common, human heart of us all, and, oh, Lord God, let us forget not to be kind.

Some of the early club programs in the 1950s included "Aluminum Foil in Baking," which was a report on the uses of foil, "Vicara, a new fiber made from field corn," and "Plastics in the Home." The minutes state, "Manufacturers predict an almost unlimited future for plastics." On April 15, 1953, Gertrude Sunderlin presented "Homemade Mixes," regarding the work her students were doing on Master Mix. On January 19, 1955, the program was on "New Foods" and featured TV dinners, fish sticks, dehydrated cream, and a "refrigerator size watermelon." In 1959, a program discussed "Why Women Work outside the Home." Several programs covered nutrition and living arrangements for senior citizens. These were new needs and ideas at the time, as the population was living longer. In 1961, Mary gave a presentation on "New Developments in Housing." She said that picture telephones were a thing of the future. As if predicting the Home Shopping Network, Mary explained that in the future, "You can talk to a store, see demonstrations on TV, and make purchases by phone." She also said that washing machines would be outdated, and dirt would be vibrated off clothing with sound waves. In addition, with electronic cooking, cooks would be able to bake a potato in three minutes. Most of Mary's predictions have come to pass. In 1966, Marybelle H. Clark, a professor in the Department of Clothing and Textiles at Purdue, presented "New Materials in Clothing" and showed the club members paper dresses that cost $1.25 and, of course, were disposable.

Many of the minutes ended with the words, "Delicious refreshments were served by the hostess with Miss Matthews pouring." One can see Mary standing at the serving table in all her glory, pouring from a silver teapot. The Mary L. Matthews Club was an avenue for Mary to continue to learn, teach, organize, and socialize with like-minded women through her retirement years. The meeting held on May 15, 1968, was Mary's last. The minutes from that day state, "Miss Matthews presided at the attractively decorated tea table. The centerpiece was beautiful and unusual. Fashioned like a maypole, white and yellow mums, irises were used." Mary introduced the speaker who talked on "The Fascination of Gardening."

Mary Lockwood Matthews died on June 5, 1968, after a one-month illness. She was eighty-five. Her passing came five months after that of Lella Gaddis. Two weeks after Mary's death, the next Mary L. Matthews Club meeting took place, which was the annual picnic at a member's "lovely country home." Business was as usual for the most part, although the minutes state that a bill from Wright Flowers would be forthcoming for flowers for Mary's funeral. To commemorate Mary's birthday, it was voted that the club would give every October 13 to the Mary L. Matthews Scholarship Fund established at Purdue University. Memorial resolutions and a club tribute were read as eighteen members of the club stood in the country air.

The last pages of the original book that holds the Mary L. Matthews Club minutes ends with the death of its leader. Fate had neatly packaged the sixteen years Mary had presided over the club bearing her name in one leather-bound volume. Yet the club continues today. In 2010, the oldest member is Dean Emeritus Eva Goble, age one hundred. The minutes from the end of the Mary L. Matthews Club book read:

In Memoriam
(Excerpt)

The bell has tolled for the Mary L. Matthews Club. The Grim Reaper has removed from our midst the eminent Dean Mary L. Matthews, June 8, 1968.

She was a shrewd advisor and her sterling character was a challenge to all who knew her. She was the stimulus power behind the School of Home Economics, Purdue University.

–Gladys Thomas, President, Mary L. Matthews Club, 1968

Mary was buried in Springvale Cemetery on State Road 25, Lafayette, Indiana. The career paths of Mary and Lella had been divided nearly fifty-five years before their deaths. Yet most of their lives they worked determinedly in the same direction to educate women and advance Purdue University.

As if a final nod to their shared aims, in 1968, they were buried on common ground.

Voice

Home economics extension at Purdue returned to the School of Home Economics in 1967, a year before Mary Lockwood Matthews and Lella Reed Gaddis passed away. The women who were home demonstration agents at that time loaded up their cars and trucks and moved their desks, papers, and files from the School of Agriculture on the south side of State Street, to the School of Home Economics on the north side.

Dean Emeritus Eva Goble was in charge of the move. She said, "The specialists were very agreeable. They thought they'd get better information, quicker. The home economics school was very agreeable because everybody got a bigger pension, because they had more money in the Home Ec Department than the Ag Department." Earl Butz was the dean of the School of Agriculture at the time.

The move of home economics extension from agriculture departments to home economics departments was a national wave. Cornell University was one of the first to make the shift. The transfer made sense because the country had changed. Farming had been the backbone of America, but by the late 1960s, consumerism was taking hold. Instead of the farm, the free choice of consumers was dictating the economic structure of our society. The role of the home demonstration agent had changed to help women with business issues, stress, balancing work and family, and so much more beyond preserving food and stretching a leftover. In 1976, the School of Home Economics was renamed the College of Consumer and Family Sciences to further reflect the changes in American culture. The school metamorphosed again in 2010 and merged into the new College of Health and Human Sciences. Now, extension agents are referred to as "educators." Goble said of the latest change she witnessed at age one hundred, "Today, it's about health. It makes sense. It's the future."

❧❧❧

For nearly six months near the end of the life of Kate Gaddis, she did not have a voice. She could not speak from July through December of 1945. As the atomic bombs were dropped on Japan and World War II ended, Kate sat at her library window and wondered about her life. She was already struggling with the residual effects of diabetes and a thyroid condition. Her diary was her confident. She records:

> July 16: My voice does not seem any better. I wonder if it will ever be normal.

> July 18: Am going to see Dr. Coyner tomorrow. Hope he can help my voice. I get so discouraged about it. Lella says it will be ok.

> August 15: How I did love to sing, and now I can't even talk out loud.

> August 18: Oh, I do so worry about my voice. I am afraid I never will talk again. I try not to worry Lella. Tomorrow is my birthday. What then?

> August 19: The one gift I wanted was my voice, which I did not get.

> September 5: I don't think I ever will have a voice. What have I done to cause this added affliction?

Kate's diaries have given a voice to her sister, Lella, and in part, to Mary Matthews. On a personal level, she articulated an earlier time for women at Purdue and in America. To whom was Kate writing each time she sat with her line-a-day diary and jotted down glimmers of her life from 1906 to 1946? Was she writing to her inner self to sort through and make sense of her private world and the world at large? Now Kate's thoughts are part of a greater historical whole. Her belated birthday gift has arrived. Kate's voice is bigger than she would have dared to dream—clear and so very powerful.

Index